AF711934

The Cookbook II

Worcester
Art Museum

Worcester Art Museum
55 Salisbury Street
Worcester, Massachusetts
01609-3196

© 1985 by the Worcester Art Museum
All rights reserved. Published in 1985
Printed in the United States of America

ISBN 0-936042-40-0

Editors: Gaye L. Brown
Anne P. Gibson
Designer: Logowitz + Moore Design Associates
Photographer: Ron White
Typesetter: Dix Type Inc.
Printer: LaVigne Press, Inc.

The Cookbook II Committee

Chairmen
Rebecca Crocker
Sarah Cederbaum Ribeiro

Patricia Bagg
Marjorie Bernstein
Jeannette Bonneau
Isabel Carleton
William Carleton
Polly Cushman
Kim Cutler
Arleen Danford
Marianne Gibson
Margaret Heald
Jane Heath
Joyce Jackson
MaryAnn Kennedy
Diane Kunkler
Gale Morgan
Marjorie Morgan
Mary Pantano
Naomi Slyder
Linda Vadasz
Judith Vander Salm
Donna Wilhelmsen

Cover:
Still Life
Emil Carlsen (American 1853–1932)
Oil on canvas, 38 x 45.4 cm
Museum purchase, 1914.20

Contents

Still Life, 1929
Louis Lozowick
(American 1892–1973)
Lithograph, 26 x 33.3 cm
Museum purchase, 1929.111

Preface

We're following in the footsteps of a culinary classic, the original *CookBook*, which boasts the astounding success of eight printings in as many years. Our challenge was to create a book not only with the same standard of excellence, but also with its own fresh and unique flavor. Many of these recipes cultivate the pleasures of cooking and demonstrate New England's rich blend of ethnic traditions. The recipes were submitted as special favorites that range from the simple to the fancy. A select few were translated and adapted from European recipes, many are family heirlooms, and others are new derivations of yesterday's creations.

The chairmen are grateful to the many individuals who have made the publication of *The Cookbook II* possible. We extend our thanks to the staff of the museum who offered enthusiastic, tireless commitment and professional guidance, and finally to our Trustees and director, Tom L. Freudenheim, whose final vote of confidence insured this culinary masterpiece a place in your home.

In addition, we would like to thank the following artists and representatives who have given us permission to reproduce their works from our collection in this volume: ACA Galleries, New York, for Roy Carruthers; Leonard Baskin; Riva Blumenfeld, for Linda Plotkin; Muldoon Elder, Vorpal, for Yozo Hamaguchi; Alan Fink, Alpha Gallery, for Peter Plamondon; August Sander Archives/Sander Gallery, New York; Sique Spence, Nancy Hoffman Gallery, for Don Nice; Ralph Steiner; Allison Stone, the Allan Stone Gallery, for Richard Estes; Brett Weston; and Helen Wright, for Henri Cartier-Bresson.

Now the challenge is yours. From the several hundred recipes submitted by members, friends, and staff, 355 of the very best were selected for your delectation. Having tested, tasted, and screened each one with our committee of scrupulous volunteers, we are sure that a cooking adventure awaits you.

Rebecca B. Crocker
Sarah Cederbaum Ribeiro
Chairmen, *The Cookbook II* Committee

Plate
French, Palissy ware
Ceramic, 24.4 cm diameter
Museum purchase, 1936.3

Appetizers

◆

Salmon Puffs

"Puffs may be used with many fillings; keep on hand in the freezer."
Mrs. Joseph C. Oakley

Yield: about 48
Bake: 20 to 25 minutes at 400°F

Puffs

- 1 cup water
- ½ cup butter
- 1 tablespoon soy sauce
- 1 cup flour
- ¼ teaspoon salt
- 4 eggs

Filling

- 1 15½-ounce can salmon
- 1 cup shredded Cheddar cheese
- 1 cup diced celery
- ⅔ cup mayonnaise
- ¼ cup chopped green onion
- ¼ cup ketchup
- ½ teaspoon dill weed

To make puffs, bring water, butter, and soy sauce to a boil. Stir in flour and salt. Cook and stir until mixture leaves sides of pan and forms ball. Remove from heat. Cool to lukewarm. Add eggs, 1 at a time, beating well after each. Drop by teaspoonfuls onto greased baking sheet. Bake at 400°F for 20 to 25 minutes. Cool.

To make filling, drain and flake salmon. Combine with remaining ingredients. Split puffs just before serving and fill. Puffs may be baked ahead and frozen. If frozen, crisp before filling at 375°F for about 5 minutes.

Prawn and Crab, from *A Little Book of Natural History*, 1951
Leonard Baskin (American b. 1922)
Linoleum engraving, 22.9 x 17.8 cm
Museum purchase, 1952.57

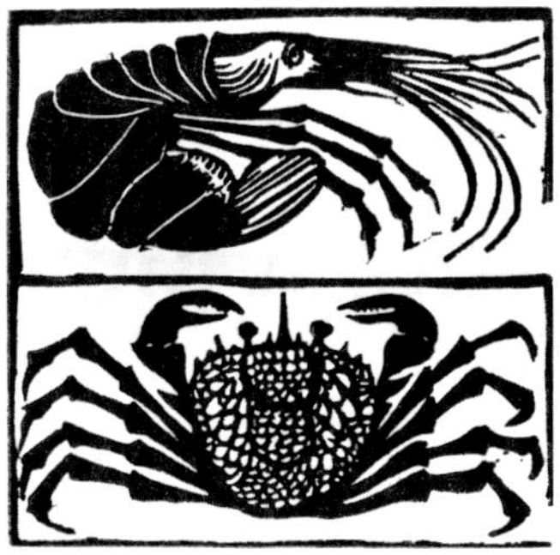

Crabmeat Hors d'Oeuvres

"These disappear immediately."
Rebecca B. Crocker

Serves: 12
Bake: 10 to 15 minutes at 400°F

- 2 6-ounce cans crabmeat
- 1 5-ounce jar Kraft Old English Cheese
- ¼ small onion, minced
- ½ cup butter, softened
- Lemon juice to taste
- 2 tablespoons mayonnaise
- 6 English muffins

Squeeze liquid from crabmeat and shred. Mix cheese, onion, butter, lemon juice, and mayonnaise with crabmeat. Spread mixture on split English muffins. Bake at 400°F for 10 to 15 minutes, until hot and toasted. Serve immediately.

Midget Cheese Puffs with Crab Salad

"To prevent sogginess, do not stuff in advance."
M. Jeannette Michaud

Yield: about 50 puffs
Bake: 30 minutes

Puffs

- 1 cup water
- ½ cup butter
- 1 cup flour
- ½ teaspoon salt
- 4 large eggs
- ⅔ cup grated Cheddar cheese

Crab Salad

- 2 cups fresh crabmeat
- ½ cup finely diced celery
- ¼ teaspoon lemon juice
- Mayonnaise

In saucepan, heat water and butter to boiling point, but do not let water actually boil. Add flour and salt all at once and stir vigorously until mixture is well blended and smooth. Remove from heat. Add 1 egg at a time, stirring after each to mix thoroughly. Fold in grated cheese. Drop by teaspoonfuls onto greased baking sheet. Bake at 425°F for first 10 minutes, then reduce heat to 375°F and continue baking for about 20 minutes. Cool.

To make salad, mix crabmeat, celery, and lemon juice. Add enough mayonnaise to bind together. When ready to serve, make opening along 1 side of puff with sharp knife and fill with salad. Note: Unstuffed puffs may be frozen.

Fairy Shrimp Mold

"For a summer cocktail party."
Emma King Peterson

Yield: 2 quarts
Refrigerate

- 1 envelope gelatin
- ¼ cup cold water
- 1 11-ounce can tomato soup, heated
- 2 8-ounce packages cream cheese
- 2 4-ounce cans shrimp, minced
- ½ cup chopped celery
- ½ cup finely chopped onion
- ½ cup mayonnaise

Soften gelatin in cold water and dissolve in hot soup. Mix in remaining ingredients. Place in well-greased, 2-quart mold. Chill in refrigerator several hours or overnight. Unmold on platter and serve with crackers. May be frozen.

Shrimp Mold

"Great versatility."
The Cookbook Committee

Yield: 2 quarts
Serves: 20 as cocktail spread; 6 as supper or luncheon dish
Refrigerate: overnight

- ½ 10¾-ounce can mushroom soup
- ½ 10¾-ounce can tomato soup
- Celery salt or seed to taste (optional)
- Salt to taste
- 1½ to 2 envelopes gelatin
- ½ cup cold water
- 8 ounces whipped cream cheese
- 1 cup finely chopped celery
- ¾ cup finely chopped onion
- 1 cup mayonnaise
- 3 4-ounce cans tiny shrimp, drained
- ¼ to ½ pound mushrooms, minced

Heat soups and add celery salt and salt. Soften gelatin in cold water and dissolve in hot soup. Stir in cream cheese and blend until smooth. Add celery, onion, mayonnaise, shrimp, and mushrooms. Mix well. Pour into 2-quart mold and refrigerate overnight. Serve with sliced Syrian bread, crackers, chips, or vegetables as a dip or spread, or for luncheon or supper with salad and bread. Note: Does not freeze well.

Potato Skins

"Delicious with sour cream."
The Cookbook Committee

Serves: 4 to 8
Bake: until bubbly at 450°F

- 8 large baking potatoes
- ½ cup butter, melted
- 1 cup grated Cheddar cheese
- ½ cup bacon bits

Bake potatoes until fork tine passes through easily. Cool and halve potatoes lengthwise. Scoop out half the potato meat. Dip each potato into butter and place in shallow pan. Sprinkle with cheese and bacon bits. Bake at 450°F until bubbly. Brown quickly under broiler if desired.

Shrimp Pâté

"Smooth and scrumptious."
Rose Dresser

Serves: 6
Refrigerate: overnight

- 1 4-ounce can small shrimp
- 1 3-ounce and 1 8-ounce package cream cheese
- 2 teaspoons curry
- 2 tablespoons Worcestershire sauce
- ½ teaspoon Tabasco
- Dash cayenne pepper
- 1 10½-ounce can consommé

Drain, wash, and dry shrimp. Put in blender with cream cheese, curry, Worcestershire sauce, Tabasco, cayenne, and half of consommé. Reserve remaining consommé. Blend until smooth. Pour into 6 small ramekins and refrigerate overnight. Next morning, drizzle remaining consommé over ramekins. Refrigerate until set. Serve with crackers.

Mussels St. Helena

"Great after a day's sail."
Marshall Green

Serves: 6 to 8

- 1 pound mussel meat (2 or 3 pounds in shells)
- White wine
- 3 cloves garlic, minced
- 1 small onion, finely chopped
- ¼ cup unsalted butter
- 1 package pork Shake 'n Bake
- ⅛ teaspoon thyme

Steam mussels in white wine to cover, until well open. Save 20 large shells. Remove meat and chop finely. Set aside. Sauté garlic and onion in butter until golden. Mix all ingredients into butter while still melted, then spoon into reserved shells. Brown under broiler and serve. Note: May be refrigerated for several days or frozen before broiling.

Hot Clam Appetizer

"If any is left over, which I doubt, it's good served cold."
Mrs. John F. Reynders

Serves: 20
Yield: 3 cups
Bake: 45 minutes at 350° F

- 1 8-ounce package cream cheese, softened
- ½ cup yogurt
- 1 tablespoon ketchup
- 1 small onion, finely chopped
- ½ cup finely ground bread crumbs
- Pepper to taste
- 1 6¾-ounce can minced clams with juice

In blender, mix cream cheese, yogurt, ketchup, onion, bread crumbs, and pepper at low speed. Add clams with juice and mix well. Put in 6-inch, round soufflé dish and bake at 350°F for 45 minutes. May be kept 30 minutes in low oven. Serve hot with toast triangles.

◆

Sea Scallop Appetizer

"Use good, fresh scallops and take care not to overcook."
Gloria J. Plourde

Serves: 6
Sauté: 4 to 5 minutes

- 1 pound sea scallops
- ¼ cup olive oil
- 2 small cloves garlic, mashed
- ½ cup finely chopped Italian parsley
- Salt and freshly ground pepper
- ¾ cup dry, fresh bread crumbs
- ½ cup unsalted butter, melted

Wash scallops carefully and cut in ¼-inch slices. In large skillet, heat olive oil. Add garlic and parsley and sauté 1 minute. Add scallops, salt, and pepper and sauté on very high heat for no more than 3 to 4 minutes. Remove scallops to bowl and let stand 5 minutes, reserving juices in pan. Turn into hot baking dish rubbed with olive oil. Mix pan juices with half the bread crumbs and spoon over scallops. Sprinkle with remainder of crumbs and baste with butter. Broil 2 minutes or until crumbs turn golden. Serve immediately. Note: The best season in New England for sea scallops is January to March.

◆

Raw Scallops with Green Peppercorns

"For appetizer or canapés."
Ruah Donnelly Lahey

Serves: 4
Marinate: overnight

- 12 fresh sea scallops
- ¼ cup very good olive oil
- 4 fresh, medium limes
- 2 tablespoons finely snipped chives, or scallions
- 1 tablespoon minced shallot
- 2 tablespoons green peppercorns, including juice
- Salt to taste

Wash scallops and slice into circles about ⅛-inch thick. Put in glass bowl and add olive oil, juice of 3 limes, chives, and shallot. Lightly crush peppercorns with flat side of chopping knife and add with salt. Stir gently with wooden spoon so as not to crush scallop slices. Cover and refrigerate overnight. To serve, lift out scallop slices with slotted spoon, letting drain. Divide scallops equally between 4 serving plates. From liquid, select some chive, shallot, and peppercorn and sprinkle lightly over scallops. Halve last lime and squeeze a little juice over each plate. Serve at once, quite cold, with small forks and toast triangles. Note: May also be served as canapés on thin slices of toast, fennel bulb, or white turnip or in little boats of endive. Garnish and sprinkle with lime juice.

Herring and Apple Spread

"Traditional family recipe."
Shirley S. Burack

Serves: 8 to 10
Refrigerate: 24 hours

- 1 12-ounce jar pickled herring pieces in wine sauce
- 1 medium to large apple, peeled, cored, and quartered
- 1 medium green pepper, cored, seeds removed, and quartered
- 1 small onion, quartered
- 3 hard-boiled eggs
- ¼ cup white vinegar
- ¼ cup sugar
- 1 tablespoon mayonnaise
- Bread crumbs

Drain herring. Place in food processor with apple, green pepper, onion, and eggs and chop finely. Combine vinegar, sugar, mayonnaise, and enough bread crumbs to make desired consistency. Stir together herring and mayonnaise mixtures. Refrigerate 24 hours. Add more bread crumbs if necessary. Serve with Jewish rye or black bread.

Chopped Herring Spread

"Tastes better if made the day before."
Mrs. Frances L. Gordon

Serves: 30
Yield: 2 cups
Refrigerate: overnight

- 1 12-ounce jar herring, without sour cream
- ½ cup mayonnaise
- 1 cup sour cream
- 1 green pepper, diced
- 1 teaspoon lemon juice
- 1 teaspoon celery seed
- 1 bunch scallions, diced
- 1 teaspoon sugar

Discard juice and onions from jar of herring. Quarter herring pieces. Mix mayonnaise and sour cream. Add green pepper, lemon juice, celery seed, scallions, and sugar. Stir until thoroughly mixed. Add herring and mix again. Make a day ahead and refrigerate. Serve on dark rye or pumpernickel bread.

Artichoke and Shrimp

"Very pretty when arranged in a sunburst pattern."
The Cookbook Committee

Serves: 6

- 1 artichoke
- Mayonnaise
- Curry powder
- Garlic and other seasonings (optional)
- 1 pound small fresh shrimp, cooked

Cook whole artichoke in rapidly boiling water to cover for 35 to 45 minutes. Artichoke is done when leaves pull off easily. Drain thoroughly and let cool. Mix mayonnaise, curry, and seasonings to taste. Pull leaves off artichoke and place about 1 teaspoon mayonnaise mixture on wide end of each leaf. Place 1 shrimp (halved if too large) on dressing. Arrange in sunburst pattern on round platter. Chill for 30 minutes before serving.

Hearts of Artichoke Canapé

"Simple and delicious."
Edith E. Wilson

Serves: 8 to 12
Broil: 3 to 5 minutes

- 1 14-ounce can artichoke hearts
- 1 cup mayonnaise
- 1 cup grated Parmesan cheese

Drain all water from artichokes and quarter. Mix mayonnaise and cheese. Cover center of each artichoke quarter with about ½ teaspoon mixture, leaving ends uncovered. Place on cookie sheet and broil 3 to 5 minutes until brown, watching constantly. Do not allow to burn. Serve with toothpicks. If desired, place quarters on untoasted side of toast rounds before broiling.

Hot Artichoke Dip

"Looks like a soufflé."
Roberta L. Aronowitz

Yield: about 2 cups
Bake: 30 minutes at 350°F

- 1 14-ounce can artichoke hearts
- 1 cup Hellman's mayonnaise (no substitute)
- ¾ cup grated Parmesan cheese
- 1 3-ounce package cream cheese, softened
- Dill and garlic powder to taste

Drain and chop artichokes coarsely. Put in blender with remaining ingredients and mix thoroughly. Place in small casserole, cover, and bake at 350°F for 30 minutes until warm and bubbly. Can easily be doubled or tripled. Good served with raw vegetables, especially yellow or green squash rounds or cauliflower pieces.

Artichoke Nibbles

"Tasty, quiche-like squares."
Mrs. Rex B. McCulloch

Yield: 30 bite-sized pieces
Bake: 30 minutes at 325°F

- 2 6-ounce jars marinated artichoke hearts
- 1 small onion, finely chopped
- 1 clove garlic, minced
- 4 eggs, beaten
- ¼ cup fine, dry bread crumbs
- ¼ teaspoon salt
- ⅛ teaspoon pepper
- ⅛ teaspoon oregano
- ⅛ teaspoon hot sauce
- ½ pound sharp Cheddar cheese, grated
- 2 tablespoons minced parsley

Drain and discard marinade from 1 jar of artichokes. Drain second jar, putting marinade into frying pan. Chop artichokes and set aside. Sauté onion and garlic in marinade for about 5 minutes, until limp. To eggs, add crumbs, salt, pepper, oregano, and hot sauce. Stir in cheese, parsley, artichokes, and onion. Mix well. Turn into greased 7 x 10-inch baking pan or dish. Bake at 325°F for 30 minutes. Cool in pan and cut into bite-sized squares. Can be served hot, warm, or at room temperature. Note: May be refrigerated overnight or frozen. Reheat when ready to serve.

Marinated Vegetables

"Colorful."
Adelaide S. Bennett

Refrigerate: at least 3 hours

- 2 pounds carrots
- 1 pound mushrooms

Marinade

- ⅓ cup wine vinegar
- ⅔ cup olive oil
- 2 teaspoons chives
- 1 teaspoon tarragon
- ½ clove garlic, minced
- ½ teaspoon salt
- ½ teaspoon sugar
- Freshly ground black pepper
- 1 tablespoon lemon juice

Peel carrots and cut into sticks. Cook until barely tender. Wash and drain mushrooms. Remove stems. Cut or slice mushroom caps if large.

Put marinade ingredients into bottle and shake well. Pour marinade over vegetables and refrigerate for at least 3 hours. Stir occasionally. Drain vegetables, arrange on lettuce or cabbage leaf, and serve with toothpicks.

Cucumber Mold

"Superb, easy, light, and inexpensive."
Marjorie R. Bernstein

Serves: 15 to 20 for cocktails
Refrigerate

- 3 large cucumbers
- 2 tablespoons gelatin
- ½ cup water
- 12 ounces cream cheese, softened
- 1 cup mayonnaise
- 3 cloves garlic, mashed
- ½ cup fresh chopped parsley

Peel and grate cucumbers. Using cheesecloth, drain all liquid possible. Soften gelatin in water and blend with cream cheese. Add cucumbers, mayonnaise, garlic, and parsley. Put in 6-cup mold and refrigerate. Unmold when ready to use. Note: Particularly good served with Bremner wafers or rye bread.

Dill Carrot Sticks

"A light, summer hors d'oeuvre."
Corinne L. Peterson

Yield: 3 cups
Refrigerate: 8 hours or overnight

- 6 medium carrots (about 1 pound)
- 1 cup vinegar
- 1 cup water
- ¾ cup sugar
- 1 tablespoon mustard seed
- 1 bunch fresh dill, or ½ teaspoon dried dill weed

Pare carrots and cut into 3-inch lengths. Cook in boiling water for 10 minutes. Drain and quarter lengthwise. In saucepan, combine vinegar, water, sugar, mustard seed, and dill. Simmer for 10 minutes. Add carrots and simmer 1 more minute. Cool. Refrigerate 8 hours or overnight. Drain well before serving.

Spinach Dip

"Quick processor dip."
Mrs. Wells B. Dow

Serves: 10
Yield: 1¼ cups
Refrigerate: at least 4 hours

- ½ cup mayonnaise
- 1 3-ounce package cream cheese, softened
- 1 tablespoon lemon juice
- ¼ teaspoon sugar
- ¼ teaspoon garlic powder
- ¼ teaspoon onion powder
- ¼ teaspoon Italian seasoning
- ¼ teaspoon paprika
- ½ teaspoon salt (optional)
- 2 tightly packed cups spinach, washed, destemmed, and dried (about ⅔ of 10-ounce package)

Blend all ingredients except spinach in food processor. Add spinach and blend until smooth. Refrigerate, covered, at least 4 hours. Serve with raw vegetables, chips, or crackers.

Spinach Squares

"Easy finger-food."
Nancy L. Albertini

Yield: 60 to 90
Bake: 35 minutes at 350°F
Cool: 45 minutes

- 4 tablespoons butter
- 3 eggs
- 1 cup flour
- 1 cup milk
- 1 teaspoon salt
- 1 teaspoon baking powder
- 1 pound mild Cheddar cheese, grated
- 2 10-ounce packages frozen, chopped spinach, thawed and drained
- 1 tablespoon chopped onion

Put butter in 9 x 13 x 2-inch baking dish and melt in oven. Remove. In large bowl, beat eggs well. Blend in flour, milk, salt, and baking powder. Add cheese, spinach, and onion and mix well. Spoon mixture into baking dish and level off. Bake at 350°F for 35 minutes. Remove and cool 45 minutes. Cut into bite-sized squares about 1 inch each. Note: Squares freeze well. If frozen, reheat at 325°F for 12 minutes.

Spinach Spread

"Make a day ahead so flavors blend."
Marjorie R. Bernstein

Yield: 1½ cups

- 1 10-ounce package frozen, chopped spinach
- 3 scallions with green tops, minced
- ½ teaspoon salt
- 1 teaspoon Worcestershire sauce
- Dash Tabasco
- ½ cup mayonnaise

Thaw spinach but do not cook. Squeeze, being sure to remove all liquid. Mix well with other ingredients. Note: Will keep in refrigerator 1 week.

Mushroom Turnovers

"Perfect party fare."
Jill O. Howe

Yield: about 84
Bake: 10 minutes at 425°F

Pastry

- 3 3-ounce packages cream cheese, room temperature
- ½ cup butter, room temperature
- 1½ cups flour

Filling

- 3 tablespoons butter
- ½ cup finely chopped onion
- ½ pound fresh mushrooms, finely chopped
- ½ teaspoon salt
- Dash pepper
- ¼ teaspoon thyme
- 3 tablespoons flour
- ¼ cup cream

To make dough, mix cream cheese and butter thoroughly. Work in flour with fingers. Wrap dough in waxed paper and chill until it can be handled and rolled.

To make filling, melt butter in skillet and brown onion. Add mushrooms and cook 3 minutes. Add seasonings and flour and stir. Add cream and cook until thickened. Roll out pastry ⅛-inch thick and cut with 2-inch round cutter. Place ½ to 1 teaspoon filling on each round. Fold in half, pressing edges with fork, and prick tops. On ungreased cookie sheet, bake at 425°F for 10 minutes until golden brown. Serve immediately. Note: Turnovers may be frozen uncooked or cooked. When ready to use, bake 15 minutes at 425°F if uncooked, or warm in slow oven if cooked.

Stuffed Mushrooms

"Food processor will speed preparation time."
Marie C. Lepore

Yield: 24 mushrooms
Bake: 15 to 20 minutes at 375°F

- 2 cups shelled fresh peas, or 1 10-ounce package frozen peas
- Salt and white pepper to taste
- Pinch sugar
- 24 large mushrooms
- 1 tablespoon chopped shallots, or green onion
- 2 tablespoons butter
- 2 tablespoons Madeira, or sweet vermouth
- Lemon juice
- Melted butter
- Grated Parmesan cheese

Cook peas until tender, drain well, and purée in blender. Add salt, pepper, and sugar. Wash mushrooms and drain. Remove stems and set aside caps. Chop stems finely. Sauté stems and shallots in butter until golden, not brown. Add purée, adjust seasonings, and add wine. Dip mushroom caps in lemon juice, to prevent darkening, and in melted butter. Fill caps with purée in high mounds. Sprinkle generously with Parmesan cheese. Pour a little butter over each. Place on buttered dish or cookie sheet. Bake at 375°F until brown, about 15 to 20 minutes.

Ethereal Mushrooms

"Really is worth the time; people love them."
Ann D. Arthur

Serves: 8 to 10 as appetizer; 4 as side dish
Cook: 8 hours

- 2 pounds medium mushrooms
- 1 cup butter
- 2 cups Burgundy
- 2 teaspoons Worcestershire sauce
- ½ teaspoon dill seed
- ½ teaspoon pepper
- 1 clove garlic, mashed
- 1 cup boiling water
- 2 beef bouillon cubes
- 2 chicken bouillon cubes

Clean and trim mushrooms, leaving stems on. Put all ingredients except mushrooms in Dutch oven on top of stove. (No need to dissolve bouillon first.) Bring to a slow boil, uncovered, over medium heat. Add mushrooms. Bring to a boil again and reduce heat. Cover and simmer for 5 hours. Remove lid and cook another 3 hours, stirring occasionally. Some juice will remain. Note: May be refrigerated and reheated when ready to serve. May also be frozen.

Mushroom Spread

"Taste defies simplicity."
Mrs. H. Paul Buckingham III

Serves: 8 to 10
Bake: until bubbly at 350°F

- 1 pound mushrooms
- 2 8-ounce packages cream cheese
- Dash Worcestershire sauce
- Dash Tabasco
- Salt

Coarsely chop three-quarters of the mushrooms. Finely chop remaining mushrooms. Beat cream cheese until soft. Add mushrooms and seasonings to taste. Pour into small baking dish. Heat at 350°F until bubbly. Serve with crackers.

Whipped Herb-Cheese Spread

"Nice green colors."
Margery B. Morgan

Yield: 1¼ cups
Refrigerate: overnight

- 2 ounces Parmesan cheese
- 1 8-ounce package cream cheese
- 2 tablespoons sour cream
- 3 drops hot pepper sauce
- ¼ cup parsley
- 2 tablespoons snipped, fresh chives
- ¼ to ½ teaspoon coarsely ground pepper

Bring Parmesan and cream cheese to room temperature. Cut Parmesan into 2 pieces and cream cheese into 4 pieces. Using steel blade, mince parsley in food processor. Remove and set aside. Add Parmesan to processor and grate until fine. Add cream cheese, sour cream, and hot pepper sauce. Blend 1 minute, stopping machine once to scrape down sides of bowl. Add parsley, chives, and pepper. Mix well. Transfer to 1¼-cup crock and refrigerate overnight. Let stand at room temperature 1 hour before serving. Serve with crackers.

Cream Cheese Boursin

"A low-cost, lower-calorie version of French Boursin."
Virginia C. Raguin

Serves: 8 to 10
Refrigerate: 6 hours

- 1 8-ounce package cream cheese, softened
- 2 tablespoons finely minced parsley
- 1 teaspoon dried basil, rubbed between fingers
- 2 to 4 cloves garlic, crushed
- 1 scallion, green portion only, finely minced
- Salt and ground black pepper to taste
- 2 to 4 tablespoons whole milk

Put all ingredients except milk in bowl. Add 2 tablespoons milk and blend with wooden spoon. Add more milk until cheese reaches spreading consistency. Pack into crock and refrigerate for 6 hours so flavors blend. Serve with French bread or white or whole-wheat Syrian. Note: Calorie count can be made even lower by using low-calorie cream cheese and skim milk. Suggested herbs and proportions may be varied to suit individual tastes.

Brie en Croûte

"Recipe can be easily doubled for a crowd."
Patricia Leonard Bagg

Serves: 20 to 25
Bake: 12 minutes at 425°F and 15 minutes at 350°F

- 1 processor brioche dough (see index)
- 1 wheel (1 kilo) Brie
- 1 egg, beaten with 1 tablespoon water

Roll out 2 balls brioche dough until 1 inch larger than brie wheel. Place 1 circle on baking sheet and paint edges with egg wash. Place cheese wheel on top and cover with second circle. Pinch edges well to seal. Paint top with egg wash. Cut out leftover dough in decorative shapes, if desired, and place on top. Paint shapes with wash. This can be done 1 day ahead up to this point. Bake at 425°F for 12 minutes, then reduce heat to 350°F and continue baking for 15 minutes. Cool 30 minutes before serving.

Roquefort Mousse

"Delicately Roquefort."
Grace E. Van Tassel

Yield: 2 cups

- 1 tablespoon plain gelatin
- ¼ cup warm water
- ½ pound Roquefort cheese, room temperature
- ¼ cup heavy cream
- 1¼ cups heavy or all-purpose cream, whipped

Dissolve gelatin in water. Combine cheese and ¼ cup cream in blender. Add gelatin and fold in whipped cream. Pour into greased, 2-cup mold and chill. Unmold when ready to use and serve with vegetable sticks or crackers.

◆

Roquefort Grapes

"Refreshing and light."
Nancy Ghiglione

Yield: 70 to 75 grapes

- 2 pounds red or green seedless grapes
- 1 10-ounce package almonds, pecans, or walnuts
- 1 8-ounce package cream cheese
- 2 ounces Roquefort cheese
- 2 tablespoons heavy cream

Wash and dry grapes. Spread nuts on baking sheet and toast at 275°F until almonds are a light, golden-brown color, or pecans and walnuts smell toasted but not burned. Coarsely chop nuts by hand or in food processor. Spread on platter or shallow bowl. Using electric mixer, combine cream cheese, Roquefort, and cream. Beat until smooth. Drop grapes into mixture and gently stir by hand to coat. Roll coated grapes in nuts and put on tray lined with waxed paper. Chill until ready to serve.

◆

Pini Cheese Balls

"Roasted nuts give a mellow flavor."
Jane and Stephen Reininger

Yield: 3

- 1 cup pecans or walnuts, chopped fine
- 8 ounces bleu cheese
- 2 8-ounce packages cream cheese
- ¼ cup butter
- 1 teaspoon paprika
- 1 teaspoon Worcestershire sauce
- 1 teaspoon chopped parsley
- 2 5-ounce jars olive-and-pimento cream cheese spread
- ½ green pepper, chopped fine (optional)

Spread nuts on cookie sheet and bake at 350°F for 10 minutes. Cool. Let all ingredients stand at room temperature for 2 hours, or until soft enough to mix easily. Mix by hand or with mixer until evenly combined. Divide into 3 balls and roll in nuts. Serve with wheat crackers. Note: 6 stuffed olives, chopped fine, may be substituted for cheese spread.

◆

Sherry-Cheese Pâté

"Colorful, pungent, and tangy."
Marlene Persky

Yield: about 2 cups

- 2 3-ounce packages cream cheese
- 4 ounces sharp Cheddar cheese, grated
- ¼ cup sherry
- ½ teaspoon curry powder
- ¼ teaspoon salt
- 1 8-ounce jar chutney, chopped
- 2 scallions, finely chopped
- Sliced almonds, finely chopped

Mix cream cheese, Cheddar cheese, sherry, curry, and salt. Spread in pie plate and chill. Before serving, top with chutney, scallions, and almonds.

Anchovy and Mustard Dip

"Even people who don't like anchovies will love this dip."
Gale Y. Morgan

Serves: 16 or more
Yield: about 2 cups

- 2 egg yolks
- 3 to 4 tablespoons Dijon mustard
- 1 2-ounce can anchovies, undrained
- Juice of 1 lemon, or to taste
- 1 shallot, chopped
- 1 cup vegetable oil
- ¼ cup sour cream
- Freshly ground black pepper to taste
- 2 tablespoons capers, rinsed and drained (optional)
- ¼ pound snow peas, or other freshly cut vegetables

In food processor or blender, combine egg yolks, mustard, anchovies, lemon juice, and shallot. Mix until foamy and pale. With machine running, slowly drizzle in oil, blending until completely mixed with other ingredients. Mix in sour cream and pepper. Stir in 1 tablespoon capers. Refrigerate, covered, until ready to use. Top with remaining capers and serve with snow peas or other raw vegetables. Dip will keep in refrigerator several weeks. Note: Snow peas may be found at Chinese food stores or specialty stores when out of season.

Blender Liver Pâté

"Mild, low in fat, and tastes like expensive pâtés."
Virginia C. Raguin

Serves: 8 to 10
Refrigerate: 4 hours or more

- 1 pound chicken livers
- 1 large onion, chopped
- 1 clove garlic, minced
- ¼ cup butter
- 2 medium eggs, hard boiled
- ¼ cup sweet vermouth
- 1 teaspoon Dijon mustard
- Salt and freshly ground black pepper to taste

In saucepan, cook chicken livers with just enough water to cover, about 10 minutes, or until done. Save cooking water. Sauté onion and garlic in 2 tablespoons butter until transparent but not brown. In blender, put portion of chicken livers, onion mixture, 1 egg, vermouth, mustard, butter, and 2 tablespoons cooking water. Blend until smooth. Repeat procedure with other half of ingredients. If using food processor, all ingredients may be blended at once. Flavor with salt and pepper. Mixture should be slightly softer than spreading consistency as butter will harden during refrigeration. Pack into crocks or oiled mold. Refrigerate 4 hours or more. Serve with French bread, melba rounds, or other nonflavored toasts.

Chicken Liver Pâté

"A real gourmet treat."
The Cookbook Committee

Serves: 10 to 12
Cook: about 10 minutes

- 6 green onions, minced
- ¼ clove garlic, minced
- ½ cup butter
- 1 pound chicken livers
- 2 tablespoons cognac, or brandy
- ½ pound mushrooms, coarsely chopped
- 1 teaspoon salt
- Pepper
- Generous pinches nutmeg and thyme
- ½ cup port wine
- 2 teaspoons grated lemon rind
- 2 teaspoons lemon juice
- ½ cup pistachio nuts, coarsely chopped

Cook onions and garlic in ¼ cup butter. Add livers, cooking and stirring until lightly browned. Sprinkle with cognac and cook 1 to 2 minutes longer. Add remaining butter and mushrooms. Season with salt, pepper, nutmeg, and thyme. Cook and stir 3 minutes. Add wine and cook until juices are slightly evaporated. Remove from heat. In blender or food processor fitted with steel blade, mix until not quite puréed. Add lemon and nuts and pour into 2½-cup oiled mold. When ready to serve, unmold and serve with crackers.

Jellied Liver Pâté

"Superb variation of this long-time favorite."
Martha C. Piehler

Yield: about 1 quart
Refrigerate

- 1 envelope gelatin
- 1 10½-ounce can consommé
- 1 8-ounce package cream cheese
- 1 4¾-ounce can liver pâté
- 1 to 1½ ounces bourbon (optional)
- Dash Worcestershire sauce
- Parsley

Add gelatin to consommé. Bring to a boil and heat gently, until gelatin is thoroughly dissolved. Pour ⅓ mixture into oiled, 1-quart ring mold. Refrigerate until set. Soften cream cheese at room temperature and blend with pâté. Add remaining consommé mixture, bourbon, and Worcestershire sauce and mix well. Pour over refrigerated mixture and chill until firm. Unmold when ready to use and garnish center with parsley. Serve with Bremner wafers or other mild crackers. Can be made a day or two ahead.

Caviar Pie

"A traditional dish."
Marjorie M. Deitz

Serves: 15 as hors d'oeuvre

- 5 hard-boiled eggs
- Mayonnaise
- Spanish onion
- 1 8-ounce package cream cheese
- ⅔ cup sour cream
- 1 4-ounce jar Danish lumpfish black caviar

Chop eggs and blend with mayonnaise. Spread layer of egg mixture in 7- or 8-inch serving dish. Chop enough onion to make second layer. Soften cream cheese with sour cream. Using wet spatula, spread carefully on top of onions. Continue wetting spatula to prevent cheese from sticking. Top with caviar. Refrigerate until ready to use.

Caviar Supreme

"For a special evening."
Gale Y. Morgan

Serves: 12 to 16
Refrigerate: overnight

- 1 package gelatin
- ¼ cup cold water
- 4 hard-boiled eggs, chopped
- ¼ cup parsley, minced
- 1 large green onion, minced
- ¾ teaspoon salt
- Freshly ground white pepper
- Hot pepper sauce
- 2 ripe, medium avocados
- 1 large shallot, minced
- 2 tablespoons lemon juice
- 2 tablespoons mayonnaise
- ½ teaspoon salt
- Freshly ground black pepper
- 1 cup sour cream
- ¼ cup minced onion
- 1 3½- or 4-ounce jar black or red caviar
- Lemon juice

Line bottom of 1-quart soufflé dish with foil extending 4 inches beyond rim of dish on 2 sides. Foil extensions will be used later to aid unmolding. Soften gelatin in cold water in measuring cup. Liquefy gelatin by setting cup in pan of hot water. Combine eggs, parsley, green onion, salt, pepper, and dash hot pepper sauce with 1 tablespoon gelatin. Taste and adjust seasoning. Neatly spread egg mixture into prepared dish with spatula, smoothing top. Wipe any egg mixture from foil with paper towel. Purée 1 avocado and dice the other. Immediately combine with shallot, lemon juice, mayonnaise, salt, pepper, dash hot pepper sauce, and 1 tablespoon gelatin. Taste and adjust seasoning. Gently spread mixture evenly over egg layer. Mix sour cream, onion, and remaining gelatin. Spread carefully over avocado layer. Cover dish tightly with plastic wrap and refrigerate overnight.

Just before serving, place caviar in fine sieve and rinse gently under cold running water. Sprinkle with lemon juice. Drain. Lift mold out of dish using foil extensions as handles. Transfer mold to serving dish using wide spatula. Spread caviar over top. Serve with thin slices of dark pumpernickel bread.

Caviar Mousse

"Can easily be doubled."
Mimi Grenier

Serves: 6
Refrigerate

- ½ envelope unflavored gelatin
- ¼ cup lime juice, heated
- ¼ cup finely chopped scallions
- 2 hard-boiled eggs, finely chopped
- Parsley, finely chopped to taste
- 2 tablespoons mayonnaise or sour cream
- 1 4-ounce jar caviar or lumpfish, rinsed

Dissolve gelatin in lime juice. Add scallions, eggs, parsley, mayonnaise, and caviar. Refrigerate until ready to use. Serve with toasted bread points or unsalted crackers.

◆

Glazed Lamb Meatballs

"Pleasant change from the usual meatball."
Mrs. Thomas R. Mountain

Yield: 50
Sauté: 5 to 10 minutes
Bake: until hot at 350°F

- ¾ pound ground lamb
- ⅓ cup milk
- ¼ cup dry white wine
- ⅓ cup minced onion
- ½ cup seasoned, dry bread crumbs
- ½ 5-ounce can water chestnuts, finely chopped
- ½ beaten egg
- ½ teaspoon salt
- ⅛ teaspoon mace
- ⅛ teaspoon allspice
- 2 teaspoons olive oil

Glaze

- ¼ cup prepared mustard
- ¼ cup honey

Combine all ingredients except oil. Mix well and refrigerate until chilled enough for easy handling. Shape mixture into 1-inch balls. Brown gently in oil over medium heat. If desired, refrigerate or freeze until ready to use.

To make glaze, combine mustard and honey in small pan over low heat. In oven-proof dish, pour glaze over meatballs, making sure all are coated. Reheat at 350°F before serving.

◆

Steak Tartare à la Suédoise

"Also delicious cooked as rare hamburgers."
Margareta G. Berg

Serves: 20 to 25

- 2 pounds ground round beef, very fresh, preferably ground twice
- ¾ cup finely chopped onion
- ½ cup finely chopped pickled beets
- 1 egg yolk
- 1 tablespoon capers
- Salt and freshly ground pepper

Mix all ingredients. Pack in bowl. Unmold onto platter and serve with pumpernickel bread rounds.

◆

Strawberries Liberté

"A unique combination."
Jeannette M. Bonneau

Yield: 6

- 6 large strawberries
- 1 4-ounce jar black caviar
- 6 slices lime
- Vodka

Select biggest, firmest, ripe strawberries available. Cut small slice from tip so that berry stands upright. With demitasse spoon or narrow, sharp knife, hollow out stem end of each berry and fill cavities with black caviar. Stand each berry on slice of lime and sprinkle with vodka.

Broccoli-Cheese Dip

"Keep ingredients on hand for last-minute entertaining."
The Cookbook Committee

Yield: about 1 quart
Bake: until hot at 350°F

- 1 10-ounce package frozen, chopped broccoli
- 1 medium onion, finely chopped
- 3 stalks celery, finely chopped
- 2 tablespoons butter
- 1 10¾-ounce can cream-of-mushroom soup
- 1 5-ounce jar Kraft Old English cheese
- Worcestershire sauce
- Tabasco

Cook broccoli and drain well. In saucepan, sauté onion and celery in butter. Add broccoli, soup, and cheese. Season to taste with Worcestershire sauce and Tabasco. Place in 1-quart serving casserole. Bake at 350°F until hot. Serve with tortilla chips.

Baked Appetizer Pie

"A real crowd-pleaser."
Mrs. Stanley R. Morton

Serves: 8
Bake: 20 minutes at 350°F

- 1 8-ounce package cream cheese, softened
- 2 tablespoons milk
- 1 2½-ounce package sliced dried beef, finely chopped
- 3 tablespoons minced onion
- 2 tablespoons chopped green pepper
- ⅛ teaspoon pepper
- ½ cup sour cream
- ¼ cup coarsely chopped walnuts

Blend cheese with milk. Stir in beef, onion, green pepper, and pepper. Mix well. Stir in sour cream. Spoon mixture into shallow baking dish and sprinkle top with walnuts. Bake at 350°F for 20 minutes until bubbly. Serve hot with assorted crackers.

Sweet-and-Sour Chicken Wings

"A tangy blend of flavors."
Wendy I. Kelly

Yield: 50 pieces
Refrigerate: overnight
Bake: 45 minutes at 350°F

- 25 chicken wings

Marinade

- 1 cup soy sauce
- 1 cup water
- ¼ cup sugar
- ¼ cup corn oil
- 1 clove garlic, mashed
- 1 teaspoon ground ginger
- ¼ cup pineapple juice

Cut off and discard tips of wings. Halve each wing at joint.

To make marinade, combine all ingredients. Place wings in single layer in large shallow pan. Cover with marinade and refrigerate overnight, turning once. Before serving, place chicken pieces, without marinade, in single layer in large shallow pan. Bake uncovered at 350°F for 45 minutes until tender and browned.

Tex-Mex Dip

"The layered taste sensation. Dig deep!"
Mrs. Saundra B. Lane and Mildred Lane Shapiro

Serves: 25

- 3 ripe avocados, mashed
- Salt and pepper to taste
- Lemon juice to taste
- 8 ounces sour cream
- ½ cup mayonnaise
- 1 1¼-ounce package taco-seasoning mix
- 2 15½-ounce cans refried jalapeno bean dip
- 1 bunch green onions with tops, finely chopped
- 3 medium tomatoes, peeled and chopped
- 1 6-ounce can ripe, pitted olives, drained and chopped
- 1 cup grated, medium-sharp Cheddar cheese

Season avocados with salt, pepper, and lemon juice. Mix sour cream, mayonnaise, and taco seasoning together and let set. In 9 x 13-inch pan or deep platter, layer in order: bean dip, avocados, sour-cream mix, onions, tomatoes, olives, and cheese. Serve with natural-flavor tostados. Note: May be made a day ahead and refrigerated.

Toasted Sweet Pecans

"An old-fashioned holiday treat."
Marjorie M. Deitz

Yield: 1 pound
Bake: 30 minutes at 350°F

- 1 pound large pecans, halved
- 2 egg whites
- Pinch salt
- 1 cup sugar
- ½ cup butter

In 10½ x 15½ x 1-inch pan, bake pecans at 350°F for 5 minutes. Beat egg whites with salt until stiff. Fold in sugar. Add pecans and mix to coat. Melt butter in baking pan, and spread pecans evenly on bottom. Bake at 350°F for 25 minutes, turning once.

Pecan Croquettes

"The chili powder adds an unusual flavor."
Mrs. Joseph C. Oakley

Yield: about 50
Fry: until golden at 390°F

- 4 cups grated Cheddar cheese
- 1 cup ground pecans, or walnuts
- 2 teaspoons chili powder
- ½ teaspoon salt (optional)
- 1 teaspoon oregano
- 4 egg whites, stiffly beaten
- Chopped pecans or walnuts

Combine cheese, ground pecans, chili powder, salt, oregano, and egg whites. Form mixture into walnut-sized balls and roll in chopped pecans. Fry croquettes, a few at a time, in deep, hot fat at 390°F until golden. Drain on paper towels. Keep warm in oven until served. Note: These may be frozen and warmed at serving time.

The Blue Bowl, 1919
Roger Fry (British 1866–1934)
Oil on composition board, 43.5 x 57 cm
Museum purchase, 1924.10

Soups

❧

Chicken and Chick-pea Soup

"An unusual and spicy soup."
Susan Josephson

Serves: 2 as main course; 4 as first course
Cook: 1½ hours

- ⅓ cup dried chick-peas, rinsed and picked over
- 4 cups chicken stock, or 2 16-ounce cans chicken broth, defatted
- ½ pound chicken breasts, skinned and boned
- 3 cloves garlic
- Cheesecloth bag containing 1 bay leaf, 1 cinnamon stick, and 4 whole cloves
- 1 small onion, minced
- 1 tablespoon olive oil
- ½ teaspoon turmeric
- ¼ teaspoon ground cumin
- ⅛ teaspoon red-pepper flakes
- 1 tablespoon lemon juice
- 1 tablespoon minced parsley
- Salt and pepper to taste

In small bowl, let chick-peas soak overnight in enough water to cover by 2 inches, or bring to a boil, turn off heat, and allow to soak 1 hour. Drain. In large saucepan, combine chick-peas with stock, chicken, garlic, and cheesecloth bag. Bring to a boil and simmer for 35 to 45 minutes or until chick-peas are tender, skimming fat as it rises to surface. Discard cheesecloth bag. Remove and reserve chicken and ¼ cup chick-peas. In blender or food processor, purée remaining mixture.

In large saucepan, cook onion in oil over low heat until translucent. Add turmeric, cumin, and red-pepper flakes. Cook mixture about 2 minutes, stirring constantly. Be careful not to burn. Add purée, bring to a boil, and simmer until mixture is reduced to about 2½ cups. Slice chicken and add to soup with whole chick-peas. Stir in lemon juice, parsley, salt, and pepper. Simmer 1 minute and serve in heated bowls.

Cold Curried Chicken Soup

"A sophisticated taste."
Elizabeth W. Ayres

Serves: 8 to 10

- 2 10½-ounce cans cream-of-chicken soup
- 1 16-ounce jar applesauce
- 1 pint light cream
- 1 tablespoon curry powder
- 1 tart green apple

Mix all ingredients in blender or food processor. Serve cold in chilled bowls. Garnish with thin slices of green apple.

Oriental Chicken-Corn Soup

"A lovely soup for luncheon or first course at dinner."
Esther C. Salme

Serves: 6 to 8
Cook: about 15 minutes

- 1 whole chicken breast, skinned, boned, and diced
- 1 tablespoon sherry
- 2 tablespoons cornstarch
- 2 ears corn
- 8 cups chicken broth
- 1 16-ounce can cream of corn
- ¼ cup cold water
- Salt to taste
- 2 eggs, lightly beaten
- 1 teaspoon sesame oil (optional)
- 2 teaspoons minced green onions, or scallions

Mix chicken with sherry and 1 tablespoon cornstarch. Cut kernels off corn. In large pot, bring broth to a boil. Add chicken and corn. Stir to separate chicken pieces. Boil 5 to 10 minutes and add cream of corn. Return to a boil. Mix remaining cornstarch with water. Add to broth and stir. Add salt and eggs and stir. Just before serving, garnish with oil and onion. Stir so oil mixes with soup.

Chinese Spinach Soup

"I've served it many times, and everyone likes it."
I. Carol Manzi

Serves: 6
Cook: about 15 minutes

- ½ pound spinach
- 1 tablespoon cornstarch
- 6 cups cold chicken stock
- 1 tablespoon vegetable oil
- 1 scallion, thinly sliced
- 1 6-ounce can bamboo shoots, drained
- ¼ pound mushrooms, thinly sliced
- ¼ teaspoon ground ginger
- 1 7½-ounce can crabmeat, drained
- 1 tablespoon sherry
- 1 cup very fine egg noodles
- 1 teaspoon salt

Rinse spinach thoroughly. Remove tough stems and chop leaves coarsely. In small bowl, blend cornstarch into ½ cup stock. In large Dutch oven, heat oil on medium-low. Add scallion, bamboo shoots, mushrooms, and ginger and stir over medium heat 1 minute. Add crabmeat and cook 1 minute longer, stirring occasionally. Add sherry and blend well. Pour in remaining stock and bring to a boil. Stir in noodles and salt and bring rapidly back to a boil. Reduce heat to medium-low and cook 5 minutes. Add cornstarch and stir constantly until mixture thickens slightly. Stir in spinach and heat until wilted. Serve immediately.

Tomato-Cheese Soup

"Easy variation on an old-time favorite."
The Cookbook Committee

Serves: 8
Cook: 5 minutes

- 1 medium onion, finely chopped
- ¼ cup butter
- 1 29-ounce can tomato sauce
- 2 cups water
- 1 teaspoon basil
- Pinch salt
- 1 10-ounce package extra-sharp Cheddar cheese, grated
- 1 cup sour cream

In large saucepan, sauté onion in butter until soft. Stir in tomato sauce, water, basil, and salt. Bring to a boil. Remove from heat and blend in cheese with whisk. Cool 10 minutes. Stir 1 cup warm soup into sour cream in small bowl. Gradually stir contents of bowl into soup. Serve warm.

Orange and Tomato Soup

"Better made a day ahead. A variation of a popular soup that can be served hot or cold."
Mrs. Paul S. Morgan

Serves: 6
Cook: 30 minutes

- 4 medium onions, finely chopped
- 1 medium potato, peeled and finely chopped
- 4 cloves garlic, minced
- 3 tablespoons butter
- 1 16-ounce can tomatoes
- Juice and grated rind of 1 orange
- 1 10-ounce can chicken broth
- ½ cup whipping cream
- 1 tablespoon sugar
- Salt and pepper

In large saucepan, slowly sauté onions, potato, and garlic in butter until soft. Add tomatoes, orange juice and rind, and broth. Simmer 30 minutes. Process in blender or food processor. Just before serving, add cream and sugar and season to taste.

Carrot Soup

"A delicate soup that can be prepared in advance and refrigerated to mellow the flavors."
Sarah Cederbaum Ribeiro

Serves: 6
Cook: 20 minutes

- ¼ cup chopped onion
- 1 clove garlic, mashed
- 3 tablespoons butter
- 3 cups chicken broth
- 3 cups carrots, pared and sliced
- ½ teaspoon basil or tarragon
- ½ teaspoon freshly grated nutmeg
- 2 dashes white pepper
- 1 teaspoon salt
- 1 cup light cream
- Parsley

Sauté onion and garlic in butter until translucent. Add 2 cups broth, carrots, and seasonings, and bring to a boil. Reduce heat. Cover and simmer for 15 minutes, or until tender. Cool and purée in blender until smooth. Add remaining broth and cream. Heat to simmering, then serve with garnish of fresh parsley.

Lentil Soup

"Well worth the effort; this soup improves with sitting and reheating."
Adelaide S. Bennett

Serves: 8
Cook: about 2½ hours

- 1 16-ounce bag lentils, rinsed and picked over
- 10 cups cold water
- 1½ teaspoons salt
- Dash ground pepper
- 5 slices bacon, chopped
- 1 clove garlic, chopped
- 2 cups chopped onion
- 2 cups sliced celery
- 2 cups diced raw potatoes
- 2 cups sliced carrots
- ½ cup tomato purée
- 2 whole cloves
- 4 cups beef stock
- 1 tablespoon salt
- 2 teaspoons wine vinegar
- 2 cups thinly sliced garlic sausage, or Kielbasa
- 1 cup sliced leeks

Cover lentils with 4 cups water. Add salt and pepper. Bring to a boil, reduce heat, and simmer 1 hour. In frying pan, sauté bacon and garlic. In 6-quart soup kettle, combine lentils, bacon, garlic, onion, celery, potatoes, carrots, tomato, cloves, stock, remaining water, and tablespoon salt. Simmer 1 hour and 30 minutes. Add vinegar, sausage, leeks, and seasonings to taste. Cook until leeks are tender.

Cheesy Cauliflower Soup

"Enticing and delicious."
Mrs. Lambi N. Adams

Serves: 4
Cook: about 15 to 20 minutes

- 2 tablespoons chopped onion
- ¼ cup butter
- 2 tablespoons all-purpose flour
- 4 cups milk
- Salt to taste
- Dash pepper (optional)
- 1 medium head cauliflower, cooked and finely chopped
- 1 cup shredded, sharp Cheddar cheese

Sauté onion in butter until tender. Blend in flour. Gradually add milk, seasonings, and cauliflower. Cook until smooth and slightly thick, stirring frequently. Add cheese and stir until melted and blended. Serve with croutons.

The Scullion (L'Aide de cuisine)
Theodule Ribot (French 1823–1891)
Etching, 24.1 x 15.9 cm
Museum purchase, 1978.50

Hearty Vegetable Soup

"While I was cooking this, the mailman stopped by the window to ask what the delicious smell was."
Kim Cutler

Serves: 8
Cook: 1 hour

- 2 tablespoons margarine
- 2 tablespoons olive oil
- 1 cup sliced carrots
- 1 cup sliced celery
- 1 cup chopped onion
- 1 clove garlic, crushed
- 9 medium tomatoes, or 2 17-ounce cans tomatoes with juice
- 1 teaspoon oregano
- 1 teaspoon basil
- 2 teaspoons salt
- Pepper to taste
- 2 13¾-ounce cans beef broth
- 1 cup fresh green beans, cut up
- 2 cups fresh zucchini, halved lengthwise and thinly sliced
- ¼ cup chopped parsley
- Grated Parmesan cheese

Heat butter and oil in Dutch oven and sauté carrots, celery, onion, and garlic for 5 minutes. Peel tomatoes. Add to Dutch oven with oregano, basil, salt, and pepper. Cook 15 minutes. Add broth and green beans. Cook 20 minutes. Add zucchini and parsley and cook 10 more minutes. Do not overcook, vegetables should be slightly crisp. Serve with Parmesan cheese. Note: Best made from summer vegetables. Freezes well.

Green Velvet Soup

"Be prepared to have your guests faint. Good hot or cold."
Ann C. Nelson

Serves: 8
Cook: 30 to 40 minutes

- 2 cups leeks
- ¼ cup butter
- 2 cups potatoes, peeled and cut into small cubes
- 2 cups asparagus, cut in ½-inch pieces
- 1½ quarts chicken stock
- Salt and white pepper to taste
- 1 to 2 cups light cream
- Snipped chives

Halve leeks lengthwise, wash carefully, and slice thinly. In large heavy pan, lightly sauté leeks in butter. Dry potato cubes and toss with leeks. Sauté again for about 3 minutes. Add asparagus, stock, salt, and pepper. Bring to a boil, lower heat, and simmer gently for 30 to 40 minutes until all vegetables are very soft. Put contents in food processor or blender and purée. Add cream and adjust for seasoning. Garnish with chives.

Senegalese Soup

"Can be served hot or cold; absolutely exquisite."
Gaye Brown

Serves: 10
Cook: about 1 hour

- ½ cup butter
- 3 medium onions, coarsely chopped
- 4 stalks celery, chopped
- 5 tablespoons flour
- 2 tablespoons curry powder
- 1 2-pound 14-ounce can chicken broth
- 3 apples, peeled and chopped
- 1 bay leaf
- ½ pound shrimp, shelled and cleaned
- 1 cup medium cream

Melt butter in large saucepan. Add onion and celery and cook until vegetables are limp. Add flour and curry and cook several minutes, stirring thoroughly to form thick paste. Gradually stir in chicken broth. Add apples and bay leaf. Bring to a boil, reduce to a simmer, cover, and cook 30 minutes. Remove bay leaf. Cool mixture slightly and blend until smooth in blender or food processor. Strain and return to pan. Add shrimp, cover, and simmer 15 minutes, stirring occasionally. Add cream and heat, but do not boil. Serve hot or cold. Note: Cannot be frozen.

Watercress Soup

"A mild, summery soup."
William T. Carleton

Serves: 4 to 6
Cook: about 5 minutes

- 3 medium potatoes, peeled and boiled
- 2 13-ounce cans chicken broth
- 1 bunch watercress, coarse stems removed
- 2 tablespoons butter
- 2 tablespoons flour
- Salt and pepper
- ½ cup cream

In food processor, purée potatoes with 1 can chicken broth until smooth. Add watercress and process until well mixed. Add butter and flour and process 10 seconds. Season to taste with salt and pepper. Process 5 seconds. Pour mixture into saucepan and add remaining broth, mixing well. Boil 5 minutes, stirring frequently, while adding cream. May be served hot or cold.

Chilled Avocado Soup

"Unusual and wonderful flavor."
Elizabeth W. Ayres

Serves: 6
Cook: 10 minutes

- 1 large, ripe avocado
- 1 pint chicken broth
- 1 teaspoon chili powder
- 1 teaspoon coriander
- 1 cup heavy cream
- 1 3- or 4-ounce jar red caviar

Peel and mash avocado. Blend avocado, broth, chili powder, and coriander for 2 minutes in food processor or blender. Heat 10 minutes in double boiler. Cool. Add cream and chill thoroughly. To serve, garnish each bowl with 1 teaspoon caviar.

Vichyssoise

"Must be prepared with white leeks and chilled properly for a real French flavor."
Mrs. Henry W. LaJoie

Serves: 6 to 7
Cook: 20 to 30 minutes

- 4 good-sized leeks
- ¼ cup butter
- 1 medium onion, chopped
- 2 pints chicken stock
- 6 medium potatoes, chopped
- 1 pint scalded milk
- Salt and white pepper to taste
- 1 pint light cream
- 1 pint heavy cream
- Chopped chives

Discard green tops of leeks, then wash and finely slice white portions. Melt butter, add leeks and onion, and cook gently until soft but not browned. Add chicken stock and potatoes and cook until tender. Purée in blender or food processor, then rub through sieve. Return soup to pan. Add milk and salt and pepper, stirring well. Continue stirring and add light cream. Bring to a boil. Add more salt and pepper if desired. Remove from heat and cool. Add heavy cream and chill thoroughly. Serve with chopped chives. Note: For variety blend in iced tomato juice, about ¼ cup to every cup of vichyssoise.

White Gazpacho

"Wonderful on a summer night."
Marlene Persky

Serves: 6 to 8
Refrigerate: overnight

- 3 medium cucumbers, peeled and cut in chunks
- 3 cups chicken broth
- 3 cups sour cream
- 2 tablespoons white vinegar
- 2 teaspoons salt
- 1 clove garlic, crushed
- ½ cup sliced scallions
- ½ cup chopped parsley
- 2 tomatoes, finely chopped
- ¾ cup chopped, toasted almonds

Whirl cucumbers in blender or food processor with a little chicken broth until mixture reaches desired consistency. Combine with remaining broth, sour cream, vinegar, salt, and garlic. Stir to mix. Add scallions, parsley, and three-quarters of the tomatoes and refrigerate overnight. When ready to serve, garnish with remaining tomatoes and almonds.

Minestrone

GOOD

"A meal with French bread and a salad."
Mrs. Michael D. Brockelman

Serves: 8 to 10
Cook: about 1 hour

- 1 clove garlic, minced
- 1 large onion, chopped
- ¼ cup olive oil
- 6 stalks celery, chopped with leaves
- 2 tablespoons parsley, chopped
- 1 16-ounce can tomatoes, cut up, with liquid
- 3 large carrots, peeled and chopped
- 2 teaspoons salt
- ½ teaspoon black pepper
- 1 16-ounce can red kidney beans with liquid
- 1 10½-ounce can beef bouillon
- 6 cups water
- 5 ounces frozen peas, uncooked
- 1½ cups cooked elbow macaroni
- 3 to 4 tablespoons Parmesan cheese, or to taste

In large, heavy pot, sauté garlic and onion in oil. Add all other ingredients except peas, macaroni, and cheese. Bring slowly to a boil. Lower heat and simmer 1 hour, stirring often. When vegetables are tender, add peas, macaroni, and cheese. Remove from heat and let stand 20 minutes.

Winter Soup

"People who hate squash and turnips rave about this soup and can't guess what's in it."
Ann C. Nelson

Serves: 6
Cook: 45 minutes

- 4 cups chicken stock
- 1 small butternut squash, peeled, seeded, and sliced
- 2 tart green apples, peeled and sliced
- 3 tablespoons minced onion
- 1 small yellow turnip, peeled and sliced
- Salt and pepper
- Pinch rosemary
- 2 egg yolks
- ¼ cup cream
- 2 to 3 tablespoons sherry

In heavy pan, combine stock, squash, apples, onion, and turnip. Bring to a boil, reduce heat, and simmer about 45 minutes until vegetables are very soft. Transfer to bowl and cool slightly. Purée in batches, using food processor or blender. Add spices and return to pan. With wire whisk, beat yolks and cream in small bowl. Add 1 cup of purée to cream, then stir contents of bowl into soup. Add sherry and reheat, but do not boil.

Peasant Woman, 1899–1900
Charles Huard (French 1874–1965)
Etching, 24.4 x 19.8 cm
Gift of Mme. Charles Huard,
1966.105

Chunky Hot Borscht

"Hearty, cold-weather soup."
Joan D. Yood

Serves: 8 to 10
Cook: 2 hours

- 1½ pounds beef chuck cut in 1-inch cubes
- 3 13-ounce cans beef broth
- 5 cups water
- 2 or 3 leeks, chopped and washed
- 3 sprigs parsley, chopped
- 2 stalks celery, sliced
- 2 carrots, pared and sliced
- 1 bay leaf
- 2 cloves garlic, minced
- ½ head cabbage, coarsely cut
- 1 pound beets, pared and sliced
- 2 onions, sliced
- 3 potatoes, pared and chopped
- Salt and pepper to taste
- Sour cream
- Dill

In 8-quart pot, bring beef, broth, and water to a boil. Skim off foam. Add leeks, parsley, celery, carrots, bay leaf, and garlic. Cover and simmer 1½ hours. Add cabbage, beets, onions, and potatoes. Cover and simmer another ½ hour. Check seasoning; add salt and pepper, if desired. Serve in bowls, and top with a dollop of sour cream and sprinkling of dill.

Curried Fish Soup

"Good for last-minute supper."
Margareta G. Berg

Serves: 4
Cook: 15 minutes

- Oil
- 2 carrots, thinly sliced
- ½ leek, thinly sliced
- ½ red pepper, thinly sliced
- Salt and pepper to taste
- 2 teaspoons curry, or to taste
- 3 cloves garlic, mashed
- 4 potatoes, peeled and thinly sliced
- 2 fish bouillon cubes (Knorr-Swiss) dissolved in 1 pint water
- 1½ teaspoons thyme
- 1 pound cod, cut in bite-sized pieces

In small amount of oil, sauté carrots, leek, and red pepper. Add salt, pepper, curry, garlic, potatoes, and bouillon. Bring to a boil. Add thyme and fish and adjust for seasoning. Simmer about 10 minutes.

Fish Chowder

"Make 2 or 3 days ahead and refrigerate."
Sallie Coe Knowlton

Serves: 16 to 18
Cook: about 45 minutes

- 1 2½-inch cube salt pork, diced
- 5 medium onions, diced
- 7 pounds skinned haddock fillets
- 2 quarts fish stock (may be purchased at fish market)
- 10 medium potatoes, diced
- 4 13-ounce cans evaporated milk
- ½ teaspoon fish herbs (thyme, savory, parsley, basil, crushed bay leaf)
- Salt and pepper to taste

In frying pan, cook pork slowly until fat melts and scraps are crisp and brown. Remove pork scraps and set aside. Sauté onions in pork fat until golden. Remove and drain on paper towels. In large kettle, simmer fish in stock until fish flakes when tried with fork, about 10 minutes. Remove fish with slotted spoon and set aside. Cook potatoes and onions in same stock until potatoes are tender but firm. Return fish and salt pork to kettle. Add evaporated milk and herbs. Refrigerate. When ready to serve, reheat, but do not boil. Season with salt and pepper.

Portuguese Fish Soup

"Gather the vegetables from your summer garden."
Sarah Cederbaum Ribeiro

Serves: 8

- 2 onions, chopped
- 3 cloves garlic, mashed
- 3 tablespoons olive oil
- 1½ pounds haddock or scrod, cut into 1-inch pieces
- 2 10¾-ounce cans chicken broth
- 2 cups water
- 4 tomatoes, peeled and chopped
- 2 green peppers, chopped
- ½ teaspoon salt
- 1 teaspoon oregano
- ½ teaspoon ground red pepper

Sauté onions and garlic in oil until onions are translucent. Add remaining ingredients. Bring to a boil. Reduce heat to simmer. Cover and cook for 5 minutes, or until fish flakes easily.

Clam and Shrimp Chowder

"Good for Sunday brunch with a spinach salad."
Terri Priest

Serves: 4 to 6
Cook: 20 minutes

- 4 slices bacon, finely chopped
- 1 onion, chopped
- 2 cups water
- 4 medium potatoes, peeled and diced
- Salt and pepper to taste
- Pinch of dill and thyme
- 2 10-ounce cans clams in water
- 1 7½-ounce can small shrimp, washed and drained
- 2 cups light cream
- 2 cups milk

In 4-quart pot, brown bacon until crisp, add onion, and sauté until light brown. Add water, potatoes, salt, pepper, dill, and thyme. Simmer approximately 15 minutes until potatoes are tender. Add clams and shrimp. Bring to a boil. Adjust seasonings to taste. Simmer 5 minutes. Slowly add cream and milk. Heat thoroughly, but do not boil.

A Carp Swimming in Deep Water
Keisai Eisen (Japanese 1790–1848)
Woodblock print, 24.1 x 36.2 cm
John Chandler Bancroft Collection,
G640

Fish

Bluefish with Dill-Lime Sauce

"A savory alternative to plain baked fish."
James Lingley

Serves: 4
Cook: 25 minutes

- 2 pounds bluefish fillets
- 1 cup dry vermouth
- 1 tablespoon minced shallots
- 1 bay leaf
- Salt and white pepper to taste

Sauce

- 3 tablespoons butter
- 3½ tablespoons flour
- Reserved fish liquid
- ½ to ¾ cup milk
- 2 egg yolks, slightly beaten
- 2 tablespoons dill weed
- Fresh lime juice
- 1 cup grated Swiss or Gruyère cheese

Place bluefish in greased, shallow 8 x 13-inch baking pan. Add vermouth, shallots, bay leaf, and salt and pepper. Add water to cover bluefish. Cover pan with waxed paper and bring to simmer on top of stove. Bake, covered, in preheated 350°F oven for 8 to 10 minutes. Uncover dish. Strain and save liquid. Reduce to 1 cup.

Melt butter in medium saucepan. Add flour and cook, stirring occasionally, for 2 minutes over medium-high heat. Blend in fish liquid with whisk, stirring until thickened. Thin with milk. While stirring add small amount of hot sauce to egg yolks. Return egg yolks to saucepan while whisking. Add dill. Heat to boiling. Thin with milk if necessary. Season and add lime juice to taste. Spoon sauce over fish. Sprinkle cheese on top. Place under broiler until hot and bubbly.

Cioppino

"Italian fish stew."
Mrs. William F. Sullivan

Serves: 8
Cook: about 35 minutes

- 2 tablespoons olive oil
- 2 tablespoons butter
- 2 medium onions, diced
- 1 clove garlic, minced
- 2 pounds fresh tomatoes peeled and chopped, or 1 16-ounce can whole tomatoes, chopped, plus liquid
- 3 cups dry white wine
- Salt and pepper to taste
- 2 basil leaves, cut up
- ½ teaspoon thyme
- 3 pounds fish fillets (haddock, cod, or scrod)
- 24 mussels or little-neck clams in shells, cleaned (optional)
- ¼ cup chopped parsley

In large pot, heat oil and butter. Add onions and garlic, cooking slowly until onions are wilted. Add tomatoes, wine, and seasonings. Cook 20 minutes. Add fish and enough water to cover. Bring to a boil and add mussels and parsley. Cover and simmer for 15 minutes, or until shells open. Serve in soup bowls.

Shrimp Kebabs

"A perfect dish for summer dining."
The Cookbook Committee

Serves: 4
Grill: about 10 minutes

- 1½ pounds raw shrimp
- 4 slices bacon
- 1 #2 can sliced pineapple
- 1 tablespoon Dijon mustard
- Juice of 1 lime
- 1 teaspoon sugar
- 1 teaspoon salt
- Pepper to taste
- Dash cayenne pepper
- 8 tablespoons butter, melted

Peel and devein shrimp; rinse and drain them on toweling. Cut bacon in squares and pineapple slices in quarters. Spear alternating pieces of each on skewers. Mix mustard, lime juice, sugar, salt, pepper, and cayenne into melted butter and brush sauce over kebabs. Grill 6 to 8 inches over medium-hot coals. Turn skewers as needed and baste frequently while cooking.

Simple Sole

"An easy fish dish for family dinners."
Kim Cutler

Serves: 4
Bake: 15 to 20 minutes at 400°F

- ½ cup butter
- 1 pound white fish fillets
- 1 cup fresh bread crumbs
- 2 tablespoons parsley

Place butter in 9 x 13-inch baking dish. Melt in 400°F oven. Remove from oven and dip fillets in butter and in bread crumbs. Put breaded fillets back in pan, sprinkle with parsley, and bake for 15 to 20 minutes. Do not overbake.

Poissonnerie
Arthur W. Heintzelman
(American 1891–1965)
Etching, 20.9 x 23.5 cm
Gift of Louis W. Black, 1955.26

Chicken and Seafood Casserole

"Serve with wild rice."
Margery B. Morgan

Serves: 10
Bake: 30 to 45 minutes at 350°F

- 4 pounds assorted seafood (shrimp, crabmeat, scallops, haddock, or langostinos)
- 2 chicken breasts
- ½ pound mushrooms, sliced
- 1 onion, minced
- ¼ cup butter
- ¼ cup flour
- 1 10¾-ounce can cream-of-shrimp soup
- 1 15-ounce can oyster stew
- 1 cup court bouillon, or bottled clam juice
- 1 cup chicken stock
- ¼ cup sherry

Cut seafood and chicken into bite-sized pieces and reserve. Sauté mushrooms and onion in butter. Reduce heat, stir in flour, and gradually blend in all liquids, stirring until thickened. Add seafood, chicken, onions, and mushrooms. Pour into 5-quart casserole. Bake at 350°F for 30 to 45 minutes. Note: For more flavor, add dry mustard, Worcestershire sauce, and tomato paste.

Curried Tuna and Fruit

"A good 'main course' for a light meal."
Gaye Brown

Serves: 4

- 1 tablespoon curry powder
- ⅔ cup mayonnaise
- 1 13-ounce can white tuna in water, drained
- ⅓ cup raisins
- 1 small apple, cored and thinly sliced

Mix curry with mayonnaise. Add remaining ingredients and mix thoroughly. Serve on lettuce or Syrian bread. Note: Flavor is best if prepared at least a few hours ahead.

Tuna Almondine

"Dresses up an old favorite."
Evelyn S. Heller

Serves: 4
Bake: 25 to 30 minutes at 350°F

- 1 bunch fresh broccoli
- Pinch baking soda and salt
- 2 7-ounce cans tuna, drained and flaked
- 6 tablespoons butter
- ½ cup blanched, slivered almonds
- 5 tablespoons flour
- 1 teaspoon salt
- ⅛ teaspoon freshly ground pepper
- ⅛ teaspoon nutmeg
- 3 cups milk
- 2 tablespoons sherry
- Paprika
- Grated Parmesan cheese

Cook broccoli with baking soda and salt. Cut off stems and arrange flowerets on bottom of buttered casserole. Sprinkle tuna over broccoli. Melt butter in saucepan and add almonds. Sauté until slightly browned. Blend in flour, salt, pepper, and nutmeg. Add milk, stirring until sauce is smooth and thickened. Add sherry and check seasoning. Pour sauce over tuna. Sprinkle with paprika and Parmesan cheese. Bake at 350°F for 25 to 30 minutes.

Salmon Loaf

"Good served with tiny peas and green salad."
Mrs. Howard G. Freeman

Serves: 4 to 6
Bake: 45 minutes at 375°F

- 1 15½-ounce can red salmon
- 2 slices white bread, crusts removed
- 1½ cups milk, scalded
- 2 eggs, beaten
- 4 tablespoons butter, melted (optional)
- ½ teaspoon salt
- ⅛ teaspoon paprika
- 1 tablespoon minced parsley
- 2 tablespoons minced onion

Mash salmon in own juice. Soak bread in milk. Combine eggs, bread and milk, butter, and seasonings with salmon. Pour into buttered, 1-quart loaf pan. Bake at 375°F, uncovered, for 45 minutes, or until top is brown.

Szechuan Fish

"A spicy Oriental dish."
Ruah Donnelly Lahey

Serves: 4 to 6
Sauté: 8 minutes

- 1 pound haddock fillet
- 3 tablespoons olive oil
- 3 tablespoons butter
- 2 or 3 cloves garlic, minced
- 1 ounce fresh ginger root, cut in thin strips
- 1 tablespoon sugar
- 1 tablespoon cider vinegar
- 2½ tablespoons light soy sauce
- 1 tablespoon cornstarch
- 6 tablespoons water
- 2 scallions, chopped

Cut fillet into 6 pieces. Heat oil and butter in skillet and sauté fish lightly, 3 to 4 minutes on each side, until it flakes with fork. Transfer to warm serving platter. Make sauce by adding garlic and ginger to oil remaining in skillet. Add sugar mixed with vinegar and soy sauce. Add any juices that have collected in fish platter. Simmer. Combine cornstarch and water and gradually stir into liquid in skillet. Cook, stirring with whisk, until sauce is smooth and thickened. Test for flavor and consistency. If too thick, add a little more water. Pour sauce over fish. Sprinkle with scallions and serve immediately.

Scallop Casserole

"A different flavor."
Mrs. Jack Magune

Serves: 4
Marinate: 1 hour
Bake: 20 minutes at 350°F

- 1 pound scallops
- ¼ cup Italian salad dressing
- ¼ cup dry vermouth
- ½ cup fine, dry bread crumbs
- ½ pound mushrooms, sliced
- 1 large green pepper, cut in small chunks

If scallops are large, cut in half. In bowl, combine salad dressing and vermouth. Place scallops in mixture, cover, and marinate for 1 hour. Drain, reserve marinade, and coat scallops with bread crumbs. Put scallops in casserole and combine with mushrooms and green pepper. Pour reserved marinade over scallops. Bake at 350°F for 20 minutes, stirring once. Brown 2 to 3 minutes under broiler. Serve on rice with colorful vegetables or salad.

Chain Letter Scallops

"A simple, fresh-tasting casserole."
Mrs. Paul S. Morgan

Serves: 4 as main course; 6 as appetizer
Bake: 30 minutes at 350°F

- 1 pound sea scallops, quartered, or Cape scallops
- 20 Ritz crackers, crushed
- 5 to 6 tablespoons butter, melted
- ¼ teaspoon garlic powder
- ¼ teaspoon Lawry's seasoned salt

Preheat oven to 350°F. Pick over scallops for bits of shell. Combine cracker crumbs, butter, and seasonings. Fold in scallops. Spoon into 4 or 6 individual casseroles or shells. In large, shallow baking dish, place casseroles in ½ inch hot water and bake 30 minutes or less. Do not overcook.

Digby Scallops

"From a fisherman's wife in Nova Scotia."
Dorothy Mayne Briel

Serves: 2 to 3
Bake: 30 minutes at 350°F

- ⅓ cup fresh bread crumbs
- 1 pound medium scallops (not small Cape or bay)
- Salt and pepper
- ⅓ cup milk
- ¼ cup butter, melted

Butter shallow, 8-inch, round baking dish. Sprinkle in half the bread crumbs. Rinse and dry scallops. Place in single layer close together on crumbs. Add salt and pepper lightly and gently pour in milk. Sprinkle remaining crumbs and pour melted butter evenly over scallops. Bake 30 minutes at 350°F. Serve at once. Note: This recipe may be doubled or tripled, but use separate pan for each pound of scallops.

Crab Louis

"Great for that special picnic or a chic evening supper."
Gale Y. Morgan

Serves: 6

- 3 tablespoons chopped scallions
- 1 cup mayonnaise
- ¼ cup bottled chili sauce
- 3 tablespoons chopped green pepper
- 1 tablespoon lemon juice
- 1½ teaspoons Worcestershire sauce
- 4 drops Tabasco
- ½ teaspoon salt
- 1½ pounds crab or lobster meat
- 3 large, firm avocados
- 2 heads Boston lettuce, chilled
- 2 medium tomatoes, cut in wedges
- 3 hard-boiled eggs, sliced

In bowl, combine all ingredients up to and including salt, and mix with whisk. Add crabmeat and stir gently. Remove skin from avocados, halve, and remove pit and brown tissues. Place avocado halves on lettuce and fill with crabmeat. Garnish with tomatoes and eggs. Note: More people may be served by chopping avocado into small pieces and arranging on lettuce. Put crabmeat on top and garnish.

Spinach and Crabmeat

"An easy, make-in-the-morning, serve-in-the-evening dish."
Janet A. Wessling

Serves: 6
Bake: 30 to 40 minutes at 325°F

- ¼ cup chopped onion
- 1 cup sliced mushrooms
- ¼ cup butter
- 1 cup sour cream
- ¼ cup grated Parmesan cheese
- 2 10¾-ounce cans cream-of-mushroom soup
- ½ teaspoon dry mustard
- ½ teaspoon Accent
- 2 7-ounce cans crabmeat, drained and flaked
- 2 tablespoons cooking sherry
- 1 tablespoon chopped chives or parsley
- 1 10-ounce package frozen, chopped spinach, cooked and well drained
- ¼ cup plain bread crumbs
- 2 tablespoons butter

Sauté onion and mushrooms in butter until onion is translucent. Add sour cream, Parmesan cheese, soup, mustard, and Accent. Heat, stirring until thoroughly blended. Stir in crabmeat, sherry, chives, and spinach. Pour into oven-proof serving dish. Melt butter and toss with bread crumbs. Sprinkle over top. Bake uncovered at 325°F for 30 to 40 minutes. Serve over rice.

Crab and Spaghetti

"A very festive dish."
Mrs. Eugene J. Ribakoff

Serves: 4 to 6

- 1 pound Alaskan king crab
- 4 cloves garlic, mashed
- ¼ pound mushrooms, sliced
- ¼ pound butter
- 1 bunch scallions, sliced
- 2 tomatoes, peeled and chopped, or 1 16-ounce can tomatoes
- 2 teaspoons lemon juice
- ½ teaspoon salt
- ½ pound white spaghetti
- ½ pound green spaghetti
- 1 tablespoon olive oil
- 1 teaspoon salt
- Croutons
- Grated Parmesan cheese
- Parsley

Drain and slice crab. Sauté garlic and mushrooms in butter about 3 minutes. Add crab, scallions, tomatoes, lemon juice, and salt. Simmer 8 to 10 minutes. Cook spaghetti with salt and olive oil according to package directions and drain. Toss crab sauce with spaghetti. Top with croutons and cheese and garnish with parsley. Note: Sauce can be frozen.

Crabmeat Mornay

"For that special luncheon."
Jane Edgington Higgins

Serves: 6 to 8

- ½ cup butter
- 2 tablespoons chopped scallions
- ½ cup finely chopped parsley
- 2 tablespoons flour
- 2 cups light cream
- 2 cups grated Swiss cheese
- 1 tablespoon sherry
- Salt and red pepper
- 1 pound lump crabmeat

Melt butter in 3-quart saucepan. Sauté scallions and parsley for 1 to 2 minutes. Blend in flour and slowly add cream, stirring until thickened. Add cheese, stirring until melted. Add sherry, salt, and pepper to taste. Fold in crabmeat. Serve over patty shells or English muffins or in fondue pot with crusty French bread on skewers.

Portuguese Stew

"A very colorful and tasty dish."
Susan F. Durham and Olive Figgatt

Serves: 4
Cook: 20 minutes

- 4 red potatoes, thickly sliced
- 1 large onion, sliced
- 4 cloves garlic, mashed
- 6 tablespoons olive oil
- 1½ pounds haddock, or scrod
- 1 red pepper, sliced
- 4 cups Swiss chard, or spinach
- Salt
- Pepper
- 1 cup white wine
- 1 jar red pimentos, drained

Parboil potatoes. Sauté onion and garlic in olive oil. In dutch oven, layer potatoes, onion, fish, pepper, and Swiss chard, adding salt and pepper to taste. Pour wine over stew and garnish top with pimentos. Cover tightly. Bring to a boil, reduce heat to simmer and cook for 20 minutes.

Haddock Casserole

"Quick and tasty."
Martha Coe Varnum

Serves: 6
Bake: 30 minutes at 375°F

- Salt
- 1 10¾-ounce can cream-of-shrimp soup
- 1 tablespoon sherry
- 2 pounds haddock fillets, rinsed and dried
- 2 teaspoons minced onion
- ½ teaspoon minced garlic
- ½ teaspoon Worcestershire sauce
- ¼ cup melted butter
- 30 Ritz crackers, crushed

Place fish in 2-quart casserole and sprinkle with salt. Combine soup and sherry and pour over fish. Bake uncovered at 375°F for 20 minutes. Stir onion, garlic, and Worcestershire sauce into melted butter and blend in cracker crumbs. Sprinkle crumb mixture over casserole. Bake 10 minutes more, or until crumbs are golden brown.

Untitled, from the portfolio *Fifteen Photographs of Japan*, 1970
Brett Weston (American b. 1911)
Gelatin-silver print, 19.5 x 21.5 cm
Jerome Wheelock Fund, 1970.141

Flounder Florentine

"Easy, elegant, and subtly flavored."
The Cookbook Committee

Serves: 4 to 6
Bake: 35 minutes at 350°F

- ½ cup chopped onion
- 1 10-ounce package frozen, chopped spinach
- 3 tablespoons instant rice
- ⅛ teaspoon rosemary
- 1 tablespoon lemon juice
- ¼ cup water
- 6 flounder fillets
- 1 10½-ounce can condensed mushroom soup
- 2 tablespoons white wine
- Paprika

In saucepan, combine onion, spinach, rice, rosemary, and lemon with water. Cover and cook 5 minutes, stirring occasionally. Remove from heat, set aside, and allow to sit 5 to 7 minutes. Place about 3 tablespoons spinach mixture on each fillet. Roll and secure with toothpick if necessary. Arrange fillets in shallow baking dish and bake at 350°F for 20 minutes. Combine soup and wine. Pour over fillets. Sprinkle with paprika. Bake 15 minutes more.

Fresh Seafood Casserole

"Serve with rice and garnish with lemon wedges."
Donna Wilhelmsen

Serves: 4
Bake: 20 minutes at 350°F

- 7 tablespoons butter
- ½ cup raw shrimp, cut in bite-sized pieces
- ½ cup crabmeat, or langostinos
- ½ cup scallops, cut in bite-sized pieces
- 2 tablespoons finely chopped onion
- 2 tablespoons sherry
- ½ teaspoon salt
- ¼ teaspoon pepper (if freezing, use white pepper)
- 3 tablespoons flour
- 1½ cups milk
- ½ cup bread crumbs
- ¼ cup grated Parmesan cheese

In saucepan, melt 4 tablespoons butter and sauté seafood and onions. Cook 4 minutes, stirring occasionally. Sprinkle with sherry, salt, and pepper. Pour into 1½-quart casserole. In saucepan, melt remaining butter, add flour, and stir with whisk until blended. Meanwhile, bring milk to a boil. Add at once to butter mixture, stirring until thick and smooth. Combine sauce with seafood mixture in casserole. Mix bread crumbs and cheese together and sprinkle on top. Bake at 350°F for 20 minutes. Note: This recipe may be frozen before baking. Thaw to room temperature and bake at 350°F for 30 minutes.

Seafood Casserole

"Easily prepared."
Nancy M. Laird

Serves: 6
Bake: 25 minutes at 350°F

- 1 cup butter
- ½ cup chopped green pepper
- ½ cup chopped onion
- 1 clove garlic, mashed
- ½ cup chopped celery
- ⅔ cup flour
- ¼ teaspoon paprika
- 1/16 teaspoon cayenne
- ½ teaspoon salt
- 2 cups light cream
- 1 10¾-ounce can cream-of-shrimp soup
- 1 6-ounce can crabmeat, drained
- 8 ounces frozen shrimp, halved
- 1 4-ounce can sliced mushrooms
- 1 5-ounce can sliced water chestnuts
- ½ cup grated Cheddar cheese
- ½ cup fine bread crumbs

In 2-quart saucepan, melt butter and add green pepper, onion, garlic, and celery. Sauté until tender. Stir in flour, paprika, cayenne, and salt. Add light cream, stirring until smooth. Add shrimp soup, crabmeat, shrimp, mushrooms, and water chestnuts. Place in 2-quart casserole. Sprinkle with cheese and bread crumbs. Bake at 350°F for 25 minutes.

Cape Cod Clam Pie

"Serve piping hot from oven."
Mrs. John F. Buckley

Serves: 4
Bake: 25 minutes at 400°F

- 4 tablespoons butter
- ½ cup chopped onion
- ½ cup chopped green pepper
- ½ cup chopped celery
- ¼ cup flour
- 1 teaspoon salt
- 1 10½-ounce can minced clams, drained; reserve liquid
- ¾ cup milk, or half-and-half
- 1 cup potatoes, cut in ½-inch cubes, cooked and drained
- Freshly ground pepper to taste
- 1 pie crust
- 1 egg yolk
- 1 tablespoon milk

In saucepan, melt butter and sauté onion, green pepper, and celery over medium heat for 5 minutes, or until tender. Blend in flour and salt. Combine clam liquid and milk. Gradually stir into sautéed vegetables. Cook, stirring over medium heat, until thickened. Gently stir in clams, potatoes, and pepper. Pour into greased 9-inch pie pan. Cover with rolled out pastry. Flute edges and slit top. Beat together egg and milk and brush over pastry. Bake in preheated oven at 400°F for 25 minutes, or until crust is golden.

Morning Glories, Black-Bordered Umbrella, and White Bantam Cock,
ca. 1833
Ichiryūsai Hiroshige
(Japanese 1797–1858)
Woodblock print, 34.9 x 17.1 cm
John Chandler Bancroft Collection,
G1471

Poultry

Stir-Fried Chicken and Vegetables

"Best made in a wok, but can use a frying pan."
Harriet N. Kamp

Serves: 4
Stir-fry: about 30 minutes

Marinade

- 1 cup chicken stock
- 2 tablespoons ketchup
- ½ cup pineapple juice
- Dash or 2 of Tabasco
- 2 tablespoons apricot preserves, or orange marmalade
- ¼ cup lemon juice
- 2 tablespoons honey
- 2 tablespoons soy sauce

- 3 whole chicken breasts, split, skinned, and boned
- Cooking oil
- 1 or 2 onions, sliced
- ½ pound green beans
- ⅓ pound mushrooms, sliced
- 1 8-ounce can water chestnuts, sliced
- 1 cup sliced celery

Combine all marinade ingredients and adjust to taste. Neither sweetness nor saltiness should predominate.

Cut chicken breasts in 2 x ½-inch strips. Marinate chicken all day, or overnight in refrigerator, stirring several times. In large wok or frying pan with curved sides, heat 2 to 3 tablespoons oil. Stir-fry chicken until opaque. Remove chicken, leaving oil and juices in pan. Stir-fry onions until slightly brown and remove. Adding more oil if needed, stir-fry beans, mushrooms, water chestnuts, and celery for 3 minutes. Add chicken and onions. Cover pan and cook over medium heat until all ingredients are hot and chicken is done, about 15 to 20 minutes.

Chicken Shish-kebab

"A nice kebab without the cholesterol of beef."
Robin D. Whitney

Serves: 4
Grill: 20 minutes over charcoal

- 3 whole chicken breasts, split, skinned, and boned
- ½ pound hot sausage
- 2 green peppers
- ½ pound mushrooms
- ¼ cup butter, melted
- 1 tablespoon sesame oil, or Worcestershire sauce

Cut chicken, sausage, and peppers into 1-inch cubes. Remove stems from mushrooms. Thread on skewers, alternating ingredients. Grill 20 minutes over hot charcoal fire, basting with melted butter and sesame oil. Serve with rice pilaf.

Chicken à la Grecque

"May be frozen or prepared ahead before baking."
Barbara L. Gavin

Serves: 4
Bake: 20 to 25 minutes at 350°F

1 12-ounce package fresh spinach
2 whole chicken breasts, split, skinned, and boned
1 tablespoon olive oil
¾ cup chopped onion
¾ cup chopped mushrooms
Salt and pepper to taste
1 cup butter, melted
16 sheets phyllo pastry

Remove spinach stems, wash leaves, and drain in colander. In skillet, brown chicken breasts in oil. Remove breasts and set aside. In same skillet, sauté onions until soft. Add mushrooms and spinach and cook 3 minutes. Season with salt and pepper. Remove from heat. Spread one sheet of pastry on a cool, damp cloth and brush with melted butter. Repeat until 4 sheets are layered and brushed with butter. Place one quarter of spinach mixture in center of dough and spread to cover an area the size of a chicken breast. Place breast on spinach. Fold long ends of dough toward center. Fold one side edge underneath pocket and other side edge over pocket. Brush top with butter and place on cookie sheet. Repeat with remaining breasts. Bake at 350°F for 20 to 25 minutes until dough is lightly browned. Serve with rice.

Sautéed Chicken with Dijon Mustard Sauce

"Elegant and easy."
Valerie Stowe

Serves: 4 to 6
Cook: about 20 minutes

1 cup flour
Salt and pepper to taste
4 whole chicken breasts, boned and halved
2 tablespoons butter
¼ cup olive oil
½ pint heavy cream
1 small clove garlic, mashed
3 teaspoons Dijon mustard
Parsley

Place flour, salt, and pepper in plastic bag and shake with chicken until breasts are thoroughly coated. Melt butter, making sure not to burn. Stir in olive oil. When oil and butter are bubbling, add chicken breasts, shaking off extra flour when removing from bag. Cook chicken on medium-high until crispy and golden brown. While chicken is cooking, combine cream, garlic, and mustard in small bowl. Transfer the chicken to a warm platter. Reduce heat to medium and add cream to pan juices, stirring constantly until sauce is bubbling and slightly thickened. Pour sauce over chicken, garnish with parsley, and serve.

Chicken Breasts with Artichoke Hearts

"Artichokes give a special flavor."
Marilynn S. Tanguay

Serves: 6
Bake: 1 hour at 350°F

- 3 whole chicken breasts, split
- ¼ cup flour
- 2 tablespoons salad oil
- 2 tablespoons butter
- 2 tablespoons flour
- 2 chicken bouillon cubes, dissolved in 1½ cups water
- 1 teaspoon salt
- Dash white pepper
- 3 tablespoons brandy
- 2 teaspoons lemon juice
- 1 cup sour cream
- 2 9-ounce packages frozen artichoke hearts, thawed and well drained

On wax paper, coat chicken breasts with flour. In skillet, sauté chicken in oil over medium heat until brown. Place in 9 x 12-inch baking dish. In 2-quart saucepan, melt butter over low heat. Add flour, stirring until smooth. Gradually stir in chicken bouillon and cook, stirring constantly until thickened. Season with salt and pepper. Add brandy and lemon juice and gradually blend in sour cream. Pour sauce over chicken. Cover dish tightly with foil and bake 45 minutes at 350°F. Remove foil and add artichokes. Cover again and continue baking 15 minutes. Good served with rice and spinach salad.

Mustard Chicken

"Crisp, tangy flavor."
Julie Martin Sanders

Serves: 4
Bake: 50 minutes at 425°F

- 4 tablespoons butter
- ¼ cup Dijon mustard
- Juice of 1 lemon
- 1 tablespoon dried tarragon
- 1 chicken, quartered, or 2 whole breasts, split

In saucepan, melt butter and add mustard, lemon juice, and tarragon, stirring until smooth. Brush sauce over chicken. Arrange pieces in shallow baking pan, skin side down. Bake at 425°F for 25 minutes. Turn, baste, and bake 25 minutes more.

Breast of Chicken in Champagne Sauce

"A dinner-party favorite."
Diane Ryan Kunkler

Serves: 4
Cook: about 30 minutes

- 2 large whole chicken breasts, split, skinned, and boned, or 4 small whole breasts
- ¼ cup flour
- 1 teaspoon salt
- ½ teaspoon pepper
- ½ cup butter
- ½ pound fresh mushrooms, sliced
- 1 cup heavy or medium cream
- ½ cup champagne

Pound chicken with meat hammer to flatten slightly. Season flour with salt and pepper. Dredge chicken in flour, shaking off excess. In skillet, heat butter and cook chicken until lightly browned on both sides. Add mushrooms and cook 10 minutes. Add cream and simmer until sauce thickens, about 10 minutes. Add champagne and bring to a boil. Simmer until sauce is reduced to creamy consistency, and serve.

Ten Spice Chicken

"A flavor of Tunisia."
Mrs. William T. Carleton

Serves: 2
Cook: about 4 minutes

- 1 whole chicken breast (about 1 pound), skinned and boned
- 4 tablespoons salad oil
- 2 tablespoons anise-flavored liqueur, or sherry
- 2 tablespoons minced fresh ginger
- 3 tablespoons thinly sliced green onion
- ¼ teaspoon dry mustard
- ¼ teaspoon chili powder
- ¼ teaspoon pepper
- ¼ teaspoon oregano
- ¼ teaspoon thyme
- ¼ teaspoon ground cloves
- ¼ teaspoon cinnamon
- ¼ teaspoon rubbed sage
- ½ teaspoon salt
- ½ teaspoon all-purpose flour
- ½ teaspoon sugar
- 1 clove garlic, mashed
- 1 teaspoon soy sauce
- Parsley

Cut chicken into bite-sized pieces and set aside. In small bowl, combine one tablespoon of oil with liqueur. Add all other ingredients, except parsley and rest of oil. Stir until mixed and set aside. In large wok or frying pan, heat remaining oil over high heat. Add chicken and cook, stirring constantly until no longer pink, about 3 minutes. Add sauce and boil 1 minute. Serve with rice. Garnish with parsley.

Chicken Muriel

"So easy, yet looks and tastes very special."
Mrs. Frederic H. Mulligan

Serves: 6 to 8
Bake: about 1 hour at 350°F

- 4 whole chicken breasts, split
- Flour, seasoned to taste
- 2 to 3 tablespoons butter
- 1 green pepper, sliced in rings
- 1 onion, sliced in rings
- ⅓ cup stuffed green olives, sliced
- 1 13-ounce can pineapple chunks, reserve ¼ cup syrup
- 16 to 18 medium, shelled, frozen shrimp
- 1 10¾-ounce can tomato soup
- ¼ cup chili sauce

Dredge chicken in flour. In skillet, sauté chicken in butter until brown. Remove to baking pan and bake, skin side down, at 350°F for 30 minutes. Turn. Add green pepper, onions, olives, pineapple chunks, and shrimp. Mix together tomato soup, chili sauce, and pineapple syrup and pour over chicken. Cover and bake at 375°F 30 to 45 minutes longer.

Thanksgiving Day—The Meal,
from *Harper's Weekly*,
27 November 1858
After Winslow Homer
(American 1836–1910)
Wood engraving, 41.9 x 58.7 cm
Gift of Robert F. Johnson, 1972.86

Chicken Cordon Gold

"Prosciutto adds wonderful flavor."
Susan Sadja Ritz

Serves: 6 to 8
Simmer: 30 to 35 minutes

- 6 to 8 whole chicken breasts, split, skinned, and boned
- ½ cup flour
- 1 teaspoon salt
- 1 teaspoon pepper
- 12 to 16 very thin slices of prosciutto (optional)
- 2 5-ounce packages Boursin cheese with garlic and herbs
- Toothpicks
- 8⅓ tablespoons butter
- 1 cup chicken broth
- ½ cup plus 2 tablespoons white wine
- ½ pound fresh mushrooms, sliced

Pound chicken breasts thin with meat hammer. Combine flour, salt, and pepper. Dredge meat in seasoned flour. Place slice of prosciutto on each breast and spread with 1 to 2 tablespoons Boursin cheese. Roll up and attach with toothpick. In large skillet, brown chicken in 4 tablespoons butter. Add broth and ½ cup wine. Cover and simmer 30 to 35 minutes. Before serving, sauté mushrooms in remaining butter and wine for 8 to 10 minutes. Add to chicken breasts. Serve over saffron rice or noodles.

Beggar's Chicken

"A rich blend of exotic flavors."
Debbie Fisher

Serves: 4 to 6
Bake: 1 hour and 40 minutes at 375°F

- 1 whole chicken (2 to 3 pounds), with liver and gizzard
- 1 tablespoon salt
- 1 teaspoon 5-spice powder
- 3 tablespoons wine
- 6 tablespoons dark soy sauce
- 2 tablespoons light soy sauce
- ¼ pound pork, shredded
- 4 black mushrooms, shredded
- 3 stalks green onion, shredded
- ½ cup daikon, shredded
- 2 tablespoons sugar
- 1 tablespoon sesame oil
- Crisco

Wash and dry chicken, inside and out. Combine salt and 5-spice powder and rub inside of chicken with mixture. Blend wine, 4 tablespoons dark soy sauce, and light soy sauce and rub over entire chicken, inside and out. Let marinate 1 hour, rubbing with marinade 2 to 3 times more. Shred the liver and gizzard and mix well in bowl with pork, mushrooms, green onion, daikon, sugar, dark soy sauce, and sesame oil. Fill chicken cavity with stuffing and close with skewers. Set aside remaining marinade. Rub skin with Crisco and place chicken in clay pot. Bake at 375°F for 1 hour and 40 minutes. Use pan drippings and reserved marinade as sauce and serve with rice.

Poulet à la Provençale

"Good served with thin noodles and tomatoes grilled in garlic butter."
Mrs. Paul S. Schwartz

Serves: 6
Cook: about 1½ hours

- ¾ to 1 pound fresh mushrooms
- ½ cup butter
- 4 pounds frying chicken, cut in serving pieces
- 1 cup dry white wine
- 2 tablespoons cognac
- 2 tablespoons tomato paste
- 2 cloves garlic, crushed
- 1 teaspoon basil
- 1 teaspoon thyme
- Salt and pepper to taste
- 1 teaspoon cornstarch
- 2 teaspoons white wine

In frying pan, sauté mushrooms in butter. Remove. Cook each piece of chicken until browned, about 15 minutes. Add mushrooms, wine, and cognac. Lower heat and simmer for 5 to 10 minutes. Add tomato paste, garlic, basil, and thyme. Season to taste with salt and pepper. Cover and simmer for about 30 minutes. (Dish may be prepared in advance to this point.) Simmer for 35 more minutes. Shortly before serving, stir in sauce made from cornstarch and wine.

Baked Chicken Dijon

"A tangy way to serve chicken."
Jean Connor

Serves: 16
Bake: 1 hour and 15 minutes at 400°F

- 4 cups fresh bread crumbs
- 2 cups freshly grated Parmesan cheese
- ½ cup chopped parsley
- 3 chickens, 2½ to 3 pounds each, cut in serving pieces
- 1½ cups butter
- 1 clove garlic, crushed
- 3 tablespoons Dijon mustard

Mix bread crumbs, cheese, and parsley. Spread chicken pieces with mixture and sprinkle remainder in bottom of shallow baking pan. Melt butter with garlic, add mustard, and stir well. Let cool to tepid. Dip chicken pieces in mustard sauce, coating well. Place in prepared baking dish and top with remaining mustard sauce. Bake at 400°F for about 1 hour and 15 minutes, basting once or twice with drippings.

Chicken Papaya

"Rich and golden."
Gail M. Price

Serves: 4
Bake: 35 to 40 minutes at 350°F

- 2 whole chicken breasts, split, skinned, and boned
- Seasoned bread crumbs
- 1 cup papaya cream
- 2½ tablespoons Amaretto
- ¼ cup golden raisins

Cut chicken into 1-inch cubes and coat with bread crumbs. Place in baking dish. Combine cream, Amaretto, and raisins and pour over chicken. Cover and bake at 350°F for 35 to 40 minutes. May be served hot or cold.

Indian Chicken

"A wonderful variation on a Middle Eastern dish."
Rebecca B. Crocker

Serves: 8
Cook: 20 minutes at 425°F

- 3 whole chicken breasts, skinned and boned
- 1 cup coarsely chopped onion
- 1 clove garlic, chopped
- 2 teaspoons salt
- 1 tablespoon powdered ginger
- ¼ teaspoon chili powder
- ½ cup drained, canned tomatoes
- ½ cup yogurt
- ½ cup heavy cream
- ½ cup flaked coconut
- 5 eggs, well beaten
- ¾ cup very coarsely ground, or chopped, cashews
- 20 sheets phyllo pastry
- ¾ cup clarified butter

Place chicken, onion, garlic, salt, ginger, chili powder, and tomatoes in large pot. Cover chicken with water and bring to a boil. Boil about 15 minutes, or until chicken is just cooked. Remove chicken, chop, set aside. Using food processor fitted with steel blade, process the cooling liquid until finely puréed. Return mixture to pot and boil down to about 1 cup. (Mixture will thicken considerably as it boils and may tend to burn. Watch carefully. If not reduced to 1 cup, remove from heat and use only 1 cup of purée.) Add yogurt, cream, and coconut. Cool. Combine beaten eggs, cooled liquid, cashews, and chicken. Lay out phyllo dough and cover lightly with damp towel to keep dough moist. Working with 1 sheet at a time that has been brushed with clarified butter, and using a 10-inch, cast-iron skillet that has been generously greased with clarified butter, layer 7 sheets of phyllo pastry, leaving edges hanging over sides of skillet. Pour in two-thirds of chicken mixture. Continue layering with 7 more buttered phyllo leaves. Pour in rest of chicken mixture. Cover mixture with 2 layers of phyllo, buttered side down. Carefully fold overhanging phyllo dough onto 2 layers on top of mixture. Using the rest of the dough, neatly cover top of pie and tuck sides in. (At this point chicken may be covered with a damp cloth and refrigerated several hours.) When ready, bake at 425°F for 20 minutes, or until nicely browned.

Chicken and Broccoli

"A one-dish meal."
Mrs. Myles McDonough

Serves: 6
Broil: 2 to 3 minutes

- ¼ cup butter
- ¼ cup flour
- 2 cups chicken stock
- ½ cup heavy cream, whipped
- 3 tablespoons cooking sherry
- 1 teaspoon salt
- ⅛ teaspoon pepper
- 6 stalks broccoli, cooked
- ½ cup freshly grated Parmesan cheese
- 12 slices cooked chicken

Melt butter and blend in flour. Add chicken stock and cook until thickened. Fold in cream, sherry, salt, and pepper. Arrange broccoli on heat-resistant platter. Cover with half of sauce. Add half of cheese to remaining sauce. Place sliced chicken over broccoli. Pour sauce over all. Sprinkle with remaining cheese. Brown under broiler for 2 to 3 minutes.

Chicken Casserole

"Must prepare the day before."
Rosamond R. Bennett

Serves: 8 to 10
Refrigerate: overnight
Bake: 1½ hours at 325°F

- 9 slices white bread, crusts removed
- 4 cups cooked chicken, cut in large pieces
- ½ pound mushrooms, sliced
- ¼ cup butter
- 2 5-ounce cans water chestnuts, drained and sliced
- ½ cup mayonnaise
- 9 3x3-inch slices sharp cheese
- 4 eggs
- 2 cups milk
- 1 teaspoon salt
- 1 10½-ounce can cream-of-celery soup
- 1 10½-ounce can cream-of-mushroom soup
- 1 2-ounce jar pimento, drained and chopped
- 2 cups buttered bread crumbs

Butter a large, shallow baking dish and line bottom with bread slices. Arrange chicken on top. Sauté mushrooms in butter and spoon over chicken. Top with water chestnuts, mayonnaise, and cheese slices. Beat together eggs, milk, and salt and pour over cheese. Mix together soups and pimento and spoon over all. Cover with foil and refrigerate overnight. Bake uncovered at 325°F for 1 hour and 30 minutes. Sprinkle bread crumbs on top for last 15 minutes of baking.

Crispy Lemon Chicken

"Especially good served with tomatoes stuffed with spinach soufflé."
Kim Cutler

Serves: 10 to 12
Bake: about 30 minutes at 375°F

- 2 cups fresh, soft bread crumbs
- ½ cup grated Parmesan cheese
- ½ cup chopped parsley
- 1 teaspoon garlic salt
- 1 teaspoon pepper
- 8 whole chicken breasts, split, skinned, and boned
- ½ cup butter, melted

Sauce

- ½ cup butter, melted
- ¼ cup lemon juice
- 2 cloves garlic
- ½ teaspoon lemon pepper
- 1 teaspoon salt

Mix bread crumbs, cheese, parsley, garlic salt, and pepper. Dip breasts in butter and roll in mixture. Arrange in shallow pan so pieces do not overlap. Bake breasts at 375°F for about 20 minutes.

At same time, combine sauce ingredients, boil for 5 minutes, and remove garlic. Pour sauce over breasts and bake 5 more minutes. Note: Bread crumb mixture may be made ahead and frozen.

Study #4, State II
Roy Carruthers
(South African b. 1938)
Lithograph
Gift of Robert F. Johnson,
1984.78

Roast Chicken with Raisin Stuffing and Orange Sauce

"Roasted chicken with a fruity flavor."
Cathy Levine

Serves: 4 to 6
Bake: about 2 hours at 350°F

- 6 slices bread, toasted, torn into pieces
- 1 stalk celery, chopped
- 1 medium-small onion, chopped
- ½ cup raisins
- 1½ teaspoons salt
- 2 teaspoons poultry seasoning
- 1 13¾-ounce can chicken broth
- 1 egg
- 1 roasting chicken, 5 to 6 pounds
- Oil
- Salt and pepper

Orange Sauce

- ⅓ cup brown sugar
- 2 tablespoons cornstarch
- 1 teaspoon salt
- ¾ teaspoon ground ginger
- 1¾ cups orange juice
- 1 tablespoon grated orange rind
- 2 tablespoons butter
- 2 oranges, peeled, sectioned, and cut in pieces

In bowl, combine toast, celery, onion, and raisins. Combine salt and poultry seasoning and mix well with other ingredients. Heat chicken broth. Add enough to moisten mixture without becoming soggy. Add egg and mix. Stuff chicken. Pour oil on chicken and smooth evenly with hands over entire surface. Sprinkle with salt and pepper. Bake at 350°F for 22 to 25 minutes per pound.

To make orange sauce, combine brown sugar, cornstarch, salt, ginger, orange juice, and grated rind in saucepan, and simmer for about 10 minutes. Add butter and orange pieces. Simmer until heated through. Pour over chicken before serving.

Parsley-Garlic Chicken

"So quick to cook, you can time your dinner perfectly."
Gaye Brown

Serves: 4
Cook: about 10 minutes

- 2 whole chicken breasts, split, skinned, and boned
- Salt and pepper
- 5 cloves garlic, minced
- ¼ cup chopped, fresh parsley
- ¼ cup pine nuts
- ¼ cup butter, or more as needed

Place chicken breasts between waxed paper and flatten with a meat hammer. Sprinkle with salt and pepper. Refrigerate until ready to use. Chop and mix garlic and parsley in a food processor, or use a mortar and pestle and mash until mixture forms a paste, about 10 minutes. Chop pine nuts and set aside. When ready to serve, melt butter in large skillet and sauté parsley-garlic mixture for 2 minutes. Add chicken and cook over medium heat for 3 or 4 minutes on each side, taking care not to overcook. Just before chicken is done, sprinkle with pine nuts and turn again. Chicken will be coated with parsley and nuts. Serve immediately, spooning remaining butter on top.

Special Chicken

"Fresh mushrooms, olives, and chicken livers make this a delicious dish."
Grace E. Van Tassel

Serves: 8
Bake: 1 hour at 325°F

- 6 tablespoons butter
- 1 pound fresh mushrooms, sliced
- 1 pound chicken livers, trimmed
- 2 chickens, 3 to 4 pounds each, cut up
- Flour
- Salt
- 1 cup canned chicken broth
- 1 cup white wine
- 1 cup pitted ripe olives, halved

In a saucepan, melt 2 tablespoons butter and sauté mushrooms and chicken livers until semi-done. Remove and set aside. Dust chicken pieces with flour and season with salt. Sauté in remaining butter until browned. Transfer chicken to casserole dish, arranging mushrooms and livers around it. In pan used for sautéing, add chicken broth and white wine and thicken with a little flour. Add olives. Pour mixture over chicken. Bake at 325°F for about 1 hour until done. If chicken seems to be getting dry, add ½ cup boiling water toward end of cooking time. Serve with noodles or rice.

Hot Chicken-Chip Casserole

"Good for leftover chicken or turkey."
Janet M. Tranquada

Serves: 6
Bake: 10 minutes at 450°F

- 2 cups cubed, cooked chicken
- 2 cups diced celery
- ½ cup sliced almonds
- ½ teaspoon salt
- ½ teaspoon Accent (optional)
- 2 tablespoons grated onion
- 2 tablespoons lemon juice
- 1 cup mayonnaise
- ½ cup grated Cheddar cheese
- 1 cup crushed potato chips

Combine chicken, celery, almonds, salt, Accent, onion, lemon juice, and mayonnaise. Put in a greased, 8 x 12 x 2-inch casserole. Sprinkle with cheese and potato chips. Bake at 450°F for 10 minutes, or until heated through.

Chicken Livers and Onions

"Variation on a classic."
William T. Carleton

Serves: 2
Cook: 25 to 30 minutes

- 1 large onion, sliced
- 4 tablespoons butter
- ½ pound chicken livers, trimmed
- ¼ teaspoon basil
- ¼ teaspoon marjoram
- Salt and pepper to taste
- ¼ cup meat stock or bouillon
- ¼ cup Madeira

Sauté onion in 2 tablespoons butter until limp, about 5 to 10 minutes. Add remaining butter and livers. Sauté about 10 minutes. Sprinkle with basil, marjoram, salt and pepper. Add stock and Madeira. Cook 5 minutes. Note: May be prepared up to 12 hours ahead and reheated.

Chicken Rockefeller

"Delicious, easy, and colorful."
Janice Harwood

Serves: 8 to 10
Bake: 40 minutes at 350°F

- 6 whole chicken breasts, split, skinned, and boned
- Salt and pepper
- 1 10-ounce package frozen chopped spinach
- 1 egg, beaten
- ¼ cup grated Parmesan cheese
- 1 cup Italian-style bread crumbs
- 3 tablespoons butter, melted

Sprinkle chicken with salt and pepper. Set aside. Cook spinach, drain, and cool. Combine spinach with egg and 1 tablespoon Parmesan. Set aside. In shallow pan, combine crumbs and remaining Parmesan. Roll each chicken breast in crumb mixture. Place in greased 13 x 9 x 2-inch dish. Place 1 tablespoon spinach mixture on each chicken breast. Sprinkle with remaining crumb mixture. Drizzle with melted butter. Bake at 350°F for 40 minutes. Serve with rice and broiled tomatoes. Note: Leftovers reheat well and remain moist. May be frozen before baking.

Duck Cooked in Clay Pot

"Start in a cold oven."
Joanne M. Zumwalt

Serves: 4
Bake: 2 hours at 425°F

- 1 duck, 4 to 5 pounds
- Salt and pepper
- 2 to 3 tomatoes, sliced
- ½ cup cognac
- 1 tablespoon flour (optional)

Soak clay pot for 25 minutes. Drain. Rub duck with salt and pepper and place in pot. Add tomatoes and cognac. Put in cold oven and set at 425°F. Cook for 2 hours. Drain fat from sauce and thicken with flour for gravy. Serve with rice.

Crispy Orange Duck

"For a dazzling effect, flame the ducks."
Carol P. Halsband

Serves: 4 to 5
Bake: 3 hours and 20 minutes at 350°F

- 2 ducks, 5 pounds each
- Garlic powder

Orange Ginger Sauce

- 1 12-ounce jar orange marmalade, or apricot jam
- 1 tablespoon butter
- 1 teaspoon parsley flakes
- 1 teaspoon powdered ginger
- 1 can mandarin oranges, drained

Clip wing tips of ducks. Remove excess fat and sprinkle skin and inside cavity with garlic powder. Using pan with rack, roast at 350°F for 3 hours, pricking skin with long-tined fork every 30 minutes. Drain cavity of accumulated fats and juices. Remove ducks to jelly-roll pan.

To make sauce, mix marmalade, butter, parsley, and ginger together. Heat until melted. Add mandarin oranges and simmer. Thirty minutes before serving, glaze ducks with sauce. Return to oven at 350°F for 20 minutes or until heated through. Using poultry shears, quarter ducks and arrange on serving platter. Flame ducks if desired. Serve with remaining sauce.

I am a Friar of Orders Grey,
ca. 1812
George Cruikshank (British 1792–1878)
Hand-colored etching, 26.4 x 20 cm
Samuel B. Woodward Collection,
1934.168

Meats

✦

Stuffed Flank Steak

"Can be prepared in morning, refrigerated, and baked before serving."
Grace E. Van Tassel

Serves: 6
Bake: 2 hours at 350°F

Stuffing

- 1 cup cooked rice
- 2 tablespoons chopped onion
- 3 tablespoons chopped green pepper
- ½ cup chopped celery
- 2 tablespoons sweet pickle relish
- ⅛ teaspoon crushed bay leaf
- ⅛ teaspoon pepper

- 1½ to 2 pounds flank steak, scored
- 1 tablespoon chopped onion
- ½ clove garlic, minced
- 1 tablespoon vinegar
- 2 tablespoons salad oil
- 1 teaspoon salt
- ½ teaspoon pepper
- Flour to dredge
- 2 tablespoons oil
- ½ cup consommé
- 6 small potatoes, peeled (optional)

Combine all ingredients for stuffing and set aside.

Marinate meat for 1 hour in onion, garlic, vinegar, and oil. Drain and reserve marinade. Lay out meat on waxed paper, season with salt and pepper, and spread with stuffing. Roll meat, jelly-roll style, and tie. Dredge in flour and brown in oil. Place meat in baking dish and cover with consommé and marinade. (Can be prepared 2 days in advance up to this point.) Cover and bake at 350°F for 2 hours or until tender. Add potatoes 45 minutes before meat is done, turning occasionally to brown. If liquid evaporates during cooking, add more consommé. Serve on platter surrounded by potatoes.

Shepherd's Pie

"A traditional English dish."
Sally R. Trottier

Serves: 6 to 8
Bake: 30 minutes at 350°F

- 2 pounds ground beef
- 1 tablespoon oil
- 2 medium onions, finely chopped
- 2 carrots, finely chopped
- ¼ cup fresh mushrooms, thinly sliced
- 1 tablespoon tomato paste
- 1 tablespoon flour
- 1½ cups beef broth
- 1 cup cooked vegetables (peas, beans, or combination of leftovers)
- 8 medium-sized potatoes, peeled and quartered
- 2 tablespoons butter
- ¼ cup milk
- ½ teaspoon oregano
- Salt and pepper to taste

Brown beef in oil and add onions, carrots, and mushrooms. Cook until carrots have softened slightly. Discard all but 1 tablespoon of accumulated fat. Stir in tomato paste and flour. Add beef broth and vegetables. Transfer to deep, 10-inch pie plate, or casserole. Boil potatoes 20 minutes, or until soft. Mash potatoes, adding butter, milk, oregano, salt, and pepper. Spread potatoes in an even layer over beef and bake uncovered at 350°F for 30 minutes.

Meatball Stew

"Simple one-dish meal."
Bernice Heald

Serves: 8
Bake: 2 hours at 325°F

- 1 pound ground beef
- ¼ cup corn meal
- 1 teaspoon mustard
- 2 teaspoons salt
- 1 egg
- ½ cup milk
- 4 carrots, cut up
- 4 onions, cut up
- 4 potatoes, cut up
- 2 cups V-8 juice
- Cornstarch
- Parsley

Combine beef, corn meal, mustard, ½ salt, egg, and milk. Shape into walnut-sized balls and brown in skillet. In saucepan, simmer vegetables and remaining salt in water to cover for 15 minutes. Place meatballs and vegetables in casserole and pour V-8 juice, slightly thickened with cornstarch, over all. Cover and bake at 325°F for 2 hours. Remove from oven and sprinkle with parsley.

Sweet-and-Sour Meatballs

"Serve on noodles or rice."
Shirley G. Ferris

Serves: 10
Bake: 35 to 40 minutes at 325°F

- 1 envelope onion soup mix
- ½ cup water
- 2 eggs
- 2 pounds ground beef
- 1 16-ounce can sauerkraut, drained and chopped
- 1 6-ounce can whole cranberry sauce
- ¾ cup chili sauce
- ¾ cup water
- ⅓ cup packed brown sugar

Combine soup mix and water in large bowl. Beat in eggs with fork. Add beef, mixing well. Shape into 40 meatballs. Combine remaining ingredients and pour ½ mixture into bottom of 13 x 9 x 2-inch baking dish. Brown meatballs in skillet. Drain to remove excess fat and arrange in baking dish. Pour remaining sauerkraut mixture over meatballs, cover with foil, and bake at 325°F for 20 minutes. Uncover and bake 15 to 20 minutes longer.

German Steak Rolls

"Recipe developed by my mother from my father's memories of a favorite childhood dish in Germany."
Beverly Runge Willson

Serves: 4 to 6
Bake: 1 hour and 15 minutes at 350°F

- 3 pounds bottom round beef
- Salt and pepper to taste
- 2 whole, medium-sized dill pickles, cut into 8 strips each
- ¼ pound salt pork, sliced like pickles
- ½ large yellow onion, cut into thin wedges
- Kitchen twine
- 2 tablespoons shortening
- Water
- 3 tablespoons flour
- ⅓ cup light cream

Have butcher cut meat into thin steaks, between ⅛ to ¼ inch thick, or partially freeze until firm enough to slice easily. Spread out steaks on work surface. Season with salt and pepper. At 1 end of steak, place 1 pickle wedge, 1 strip salt pork, and 1 onion wedge. Roll each steak firmly, jelly-roll fashion, starting at end with filling. Tie firmly through center, bedroll fashion. Melt shortening in frying pan and sear each roll on all sides. Place browned rolls in large oven-proof casserole. Deglaze frying pan with 1 cup water and add to casserole. If necessary, add enough water to just cover meat. Cover casserole and bake at 350°F for 1 hour and 15 minutes. Remove from oven. Place rolls in serving dish and keep warm. There should be about 1 cup liquid left in casserole. Add enough water to make 2½ cups liquid. Blend in flour. Bring to a boil, stirring, and simmer about 3 minutes. Adjust seasoning. Add cream to gravy and pour over meat in serving dish. Note: May be served with noodles or plain boiled potatoes.

Tournedos Sautés aux Champignons

"Elegant dish for entertaining."
Mrs. Michael J. Bradbury

Serves: 6
Cook: about 20 minutes

- 3 tablespoons butter
- 3 tablespoons shallots, minced
- ½ pound mushrooms, sliced
- 1 teaspoon marjoram
- 2 tablespoons chives, snipped
- Salt and freshly ground pepper
- ½ cup dry white wine
- 6 filet mignons, 1 inch thick
- ¼ cup brandy
- Chopped parsley

In skillet, melt 2 tablespoons butter and stir in shallots. Cook slowly for about 1 minute. Add mushrooms and continue cooking for 1 more minute. Stir in herbs, seasoning, and wine. Cook over medium high until wine is reduced to an essence. Pound steaks to ½ inch and pepper them on both sides. In separate skillet, melt remaining butter over high heat until foam subsides. Sauté steaks on 1 side for about 2 minutes, then turn. While second side is cooking, moisten with some sauce. Flame brandy and pour over steaks. When flames have subsided, remove to serving dish, top with any remaining sauce, and serve immediately. Garnish with parsley.

Baby Beef Liver à la Vénitienne

"Serve on a bed of rice."
Ann F. Gut

Serves: 6 to 8
Cook: 5 minutes

- 2 large onions, cut in narrow slices
- 3 or 4 tablespoons chicken or goose fat, or butter
- ¼ cup white wine
- 6 slices liver, ½ inch thick
- Flour and salt to taste
- Oil
- Sliced mushrooms (optional)
- Cognac
- Parsley
- Juice of 1 lemon
- Salt and pepper to taste

In covered pan, sauté onions in chicken fat over low heat. When soft and beginning to color, pour in wine and continue to cook until wine is almost evaporated. While onions are cooking, dredge liver in flour. Heat oil in separate frying pan and quickly fry liver over high heat until seared on outside. Immediately cut liver and trim connective tissue. Add liver to onion and sauté, being sure *not* to overcook. Add mushrooms, cognac, parsley, lemon juice, salt, and pepper. Serve immediately.

Resting Cows
Nicolaes Berchem
(Dutch 1620–1683)
Etching, 17.1 x 23.7 cm
Museum purchase, 1976.7

Clay Pot Argentine Braised Beef

"Do not preheat oven."
Joanne M. Zumwalt

Serves: 4
Bake: 1 hour and 30 minutes at 425°F

- 2 pounds beef round, cut 1½ inches thick
- 1 clove garlic
- 1 teaspoon salt
- ¼ teaspoon black pepper
- 2 tablespoons lemon or lime juice
- 1½ cups chopped onion
- 1 cup sliced carrots
- 4 potatoes
- ¼ teaspoon marjoram
- 1 8-ounce can tomato sauce
- ½ cup beef stock or bouillon (if using bouillon omit salt)

Soak 4-quart clay pot for 15 minutes and drain. Rub beef with cut garlic clove or chop clove and add to other ingredients. Sprinkle meat with salt, pepper, and lemon juice. Place meat in clay pot and scatter vegetables over it. Add marjoram. Combine tomato sauce and beef stock and pour over meat. Put clay pot in cold oven. Bake at 425°F for 1 hour and 30 minutes.

Zesty Meat Loaf

"A nutritious, high-protein variation."
Wilmer L. Kranich

Serves: 10
Bake: 1 hour at 350°F

- 2½ pounds ground beef
- ½ cup quick oatmeal
- ¼ cup wheat germ
- ¼ cup sweet hamburger relish
- ½ cup chopped onion
- ½ cup ketchup
- 2 tablespoons mustard
- 1 tablespoon dried parsley
- 2 tablespoons sesame seeds
- 1 teaspoon oregano
- 2 teaspoons caraway seeds
- 1½ teaspoons salt
- 1 6-ounce can tomato paste

Blend all ingredients, reserving ½ tomato paste. Form into 2 loaves 6 to 8 inches long. Place in large baking pan and top with remaining tomato paste. Bake at 350°F for 1 hour.

Hungarian Goulash

"Hearty meal for a blizzardy afternoon."
The Cookbook Committee

Serves: 6
Simmer: 2½ hours

- 2 pounds beef, cut in 1-inch cubes
- Flour, salt, pepper
- Oil, or bacon fat
- 1 teaspoon basil
- 2 cloves garlic, mashed
- 1 large onion, finely chopped
- Pinch cayenne
- 2 10½-ounce cans beef broth
- ½ cup Burgundy
- 3 tablespoons butter
- 3 tablespoons flour
- 1 tablespoon sugar
- 2 tablespoons Hungarian paprika
- 1 cup tomato purée
- Carrots (optional)

Shake meat in bag with flour, salt, and pepper, then brown in oil over low flame. Season with basil, garlic, onion, and cayenne. Add beef broth and ½ Burgundy. Cover and simmer about 1½ hours. In food processor, cream butter with flour, sugar, and paprika. Add tomato purée and mix again. Add tomato mixture, remaining Burgundy, and carrots to meat. Simmer 1 more hour.

Steak and Kidney Pie

"A classic favorite."
Mrs. Roger Kinnicutt, Jr.

Serves: 6
Simmer: about 1 hour
Bake: 15 to 30 minutes at 400°F

- 2 beef kidneys
- 1 pound stew beef
- 1 medium onion, sliced
- 2 tablespoons bacon fat
- 2 teaspoons salt
- ¼ teaspoon pepper
- 1 tablespoon Worcestershire sauce
- 2 cups hot water
- ¼ cup flour
- ¼ cup cold water
- Dough for 1-crust pie

Soak kidneys in cold, salted water for 30 minutes, and drain. Remove skin and tubes. Cube kidneys and beef and brown with onions in hot fat. Add salt, pepper, Worcestershire sauce, and hot water. Cover and simmer until tender, about 1 hour. Thicken with flour mixed to paste in cold water. Pour into casserole. Roll dough ½ inch larger than casserole. Place over meat, turn edges under to seal, and slash for steam to escape. Bake at 400°F for 15 to 30 minutes, until browned.

Sweet-and-Sour Stuffed Cabbage

"The secret to rolling cabbage easily is to soften leaves so they are pliable and roll without cracking."
Dr. Earle R. Halsband

Serves: 8 to 10
Simmer: 3 hours
Bake: 1½ hours at 325°F

- 1 large head cabbage
- 2 eggs
- ½ onion, grated
- ⅓ cup rice
- Salt and pepper
- 2 cups chopped meat
- 1 28-ounce can crushed tomatoes
- ½ cup brown sugar
- ½ cup raisins
- 6 gingersnaps
- Juice of 1 lemon
- 2 chunks sour salt
- 1 onion, chopped

Freeze cabbage. Thaw overnight, then core and steam in deep pot, about 5 to 7 minutes. Leaves should be soft and wilted. Combine eggs, grated onion, rice, salt, pepper, and chopped meat. Place portion of meat mixture on base of each leaf. Roll up, taking care to fold in sides so leaf encloses meat. Secure with toothpick. Place in deep pan lined with excess cabbage. Cover rolls with water. Add tomatoes, brown sugar, raisins, gingersnaps, lemon juice, sour salt, and onion. Cover and simmer for 3 hours. Place cabbage rolls in shallow baking dish with some broth to keep moist. Bake for 1 hour at 325°F, sprinkle additional brown sugar on rolls to glaze, and bake 30 minutes longer.

Beef and Bean Dinner

"An old family recipe."
Noreen La Salle Green

Serves: 6
Bake: 20 to 30 minutes at 425°F

- ½ cup flour
- ½ teaspoon salt
- ½ teaspoon baking powder
- ¼ cup vegetable shortening
- ½ cup sour cream
- 1 egg
- 1 pound ground beef, browned and drained
- ¼ teaspoon Tabasco
- 2 teaspoons Worcestershire sauce
- ¼ cup chopped onion
- 1 16-ounce can baked beans
- 1 6-ounce can tomato paste
- 1½ cups grated Cheddar cheese

Combine flour, salt, baking powder, shortening, and sour cream to make crust. Stir until blended, about 60 strokes. Mixture will be slightly lumpy. Spread batter thinly on bottom of greased, floured, 10-inch, glass pie plate. Spread batter thickly up sides to within ¼ inch of rim. To make filling, combine beef, Tabasco, Worcestershire, onion, beans, and tomato paste. Fill prepared crust and bake at 425°F for 20 to 30 minutes until crust is golden brown. Remove from oven. Sprinkle top with cheese and return pie briefly to oven to melt cheese. If frozen, bake at 425°F for 1 hour and 15 minutes.

Famous Chili Con Carne

"A great after-skiing meal, served with rice, tortillas, and chopped onions."
Ina F. Jaffee

Serves: 6
Simmer: 2 hours

- 3 onions, chopped
- 3 green peppers, chopped
- 4 tablespoons olive oil
- 2 pounds lean ground beef
- 1 28-ounce can tomato purée
- 1 6-ounce can tomato paste
- 6 tablespoons chili powder
- 1 tablespoon sugar
- Salt, pepper, and paprika to taste
- 2 bay leaves
- 1 teaspoon cumin
- 1 teaspoon basil
- Pinch cayenne
- 2 16-ounce cans kidney beans

Sauté onions and peppers in oil. In separate skillet, sauté beef until browned. Pour off excess fat and mix beef with onions and peppers. Mix in tomato purée, tomato paste, and all spices. Mix thoroughly and simmer for 1 hour, stirring occasionally. Add drained kidney beans and continue to simmer for 1 more hour. Note: Can be made 1 day ahead or frozen, but some of the tang is lost in prolonged freezing.

Taco Salad

"Hot and tasty."
Donna Wilhelmsen

Serves: 6
Simmer: 30 minutes

- 1 pound ground beef
- ½ clove garlic, chopped
- 1 pound canned tomatoes
- 1 can chopped green chilies
- 1 teaspoon salt
- ½ teaspoon pepper
- 1 head lettuce, torn into bite-sized pieces
- 1 cup grated Cheddar cheese
- 1 6-ounce package corn chips, mashed
- 1 cup chopped green or yellow onion
- Hot sauce

Sauté ground beef and garlic until lightly browned. Add undrained tomatoes, chilies, salt, and pepper. Simmer 30 minutes, uncovered. Before serving, add lettuce, cheese, corn chips, and onions. Mix well. Serve with hot sauce.

Greek Wine Stew

"Easy and always well liked."
Janet R. Baker

Serves: 6
Simmer: about 3 hours

- 3 pounds lean stew beef, cut in ½-inch cubes
- Salt and pepper
- ½ cup butter
- 2 pounds small boiling onions, peeled
- ½ cup dry red wine
- 1 6-ounce can tomato paste
- 2 tablespoons wine vinegar
- 1 tablespoon brown sugar
- 1 clove garlic, minced
- ¼ teaspoon cumin seeds, crushed, or ⅛ teaspoon ground cumin
- 1 bay leaf
- 3 sticks cinnamon
- ½ teaspoon whole cloves
- ¼ to ½ cup dried currants and raisins

Season meat generously with salt and pepper. Melt butter in Dutch oven or heavy kettle. Add meat and coat on all sides with butter but do not brown. Arrange onions over meat. Mix wine, paste, vinegar, sugar, garlic, and cumin. Pour over meat. Add bay leaf, cinnamon, cloves, currants, and raisins. Cover and cook over low heat until meat is very tender, about 3 hours. Do not stir. Serve over rice, stirring sauce gently to blend with meat.

Marinated Steak

"A sweet-and-sour, barbecued flavor."
Cathy Levine

Serves: 4
Marinate: several hours
Broil: 20 minutes

Marinade

- ¼ cup soy sauce
- 3 tablespoons honey
- 2 tablespoons wine vinegar
- ¾ teaspoon minced garlic
- 1½ teaspoons ground ginger
- ¾ cup vegetable oil
- 1 small onion, chopped

- 4 steaks, any cut

Combine all ingredients for marinade. Marinate steak for several hours.

Broil or grill steak for about 10 minutes per side. Baste with marinade when cooking second side.

Lamb Chop Grill

"A kind of English grill."
Margery B. Morgan

Serves: 1
Bake: 40 to 50 minutes at 300°F

- 1 loin lamb chop, 2 inches thick
- 1 lamb kidney, or 1 whole mushroom
- 1 slice bacon
- Salt and pepper to taste

Trim extra fat from chop. Insert kidney between "tail" and main part of chop. Wrap bacon slice around chop and secure with toothpick. Sprinkle with salt and pepper. Bake in preheated oven at 300°F for 40 to 50 minutes. Note: Good served with broiled tomato, spinach, and sausage.

Lamb-Pistachio Pie

"Serve with salad, fruit, and a light dessert."
I. Carol Manzi

Serves: 6
Bake: 25 minutes at 375°F

- 1 large onion, chopped
- 2 tablespoons butter
- ¼ pound mushrooms, sliced
- 1 pound ground lamb
- 1 teaspoon salt
- ½ teaspoon allspice
- 1 clove garlic, minced
- ¼ cup Parmesan cheese, grated
- 2 eggs, slightly beaten
- 2 tablespoons pistachios, chopped
- 2 tablespoons parsley, chopped
- Dough for 2-crust pie
- Melted butter

Sauté onion in ½ butter until golden. Add remaining butter and mushrooms and cook, stirring, until coated. Turn into large bowl. Brown lamb with salt, allspice, and garlic in same skillet. Drain fat. Combine lamb and onion mixtures. Add cheese, eggs, nuts, and parsley and stir to blend. Cool. Line 9-inch pie plate with dough. Spoon in lamb filling. Top with second crust and pinch edges to seal. Brush top with melted butter. Bake at 375°F for 25 minutes on lower oven rack. Cool 10 minutes before cutting. Note: Unbaked pie can be frozen for 1 month.

Lamb Shanks in Wine

"Very aromatic and tasty."
Marie C. Lepore

Serves: 4
Bake: 1½ to 2 hours at 350°F

- 4 lamb shanks
- 1 teaspoon salt
- ½ teaspoon pepper
- 2 tablespoons onion, grated
- ½ teaspoon minced garlic, or 3 tablespoons minced shallots
- 2 tablespoons oil
- 2 small carrots, cut in strips
- 1½ cups diced celery
- 2 teaspoons chopped parsley
- 2 bay leaves
- 1 teaspoon rosemary
- 1 cup red wine

Rub shanks with salt and pepper. Sauté onion, garlic, and lamb in oil until meat is browned on all sides. Place in large casserole and add carrots, celery, parsley, bay leaves, and rosemary. Deglaze skillet with wine and pour over meat. Cover and bake at 350°F for 1½ to 2 hours.

Stuffed Leg of Lamb

"Serve with rice pilaf."
Jill O. Howe

Serves: 10
Bake: 30 minutes per pound at 325°F

- 5½ pound boned leg of lamb
- 2 cloves garlic, minced
- Salt and pepper
- ¾ cup onion, chopped
- 7 tablespoons butter
- 1 cup artichoke hearts, chopped
- 2 cups bread crumbs
- ¼ teaspoon marjoram
- ¼ teaspoon thyme
- ¼ teaspoon pepper
- ½ teaspoon salt
- 4 teaspoons chopped parsley
- ⅔ cup consommé

Open lamb and rub with garlic, salt, and pepper. Sauté onion in butter until golden. Add artichoke hearts and stir. Add bread crumbs and seasonings and mix thoroughly. Spread mixture inside lamb. Roll up and tie with string. Put in roasting pan. Pour consommé over lamb and roast at 325°F for 30 minutes per pound or until internal temperature reaches 150° to 160°F for well done.

Lamb and Spinach en Casserole

"Good use for leftover lamb."
Robin D. Whitney

Serves: 4
Bake: 20 minutes at 400°F

- 1 pound spinach
- 1 tablespoon olive oil
- Juice of 1 lemon
- ½ teaspoon salt
- ⅛ teaspoon pepper
- 2 cups cooked lamb, cut in 1-inch cubes
- 1 recipe béchamel sauce (see index)
- 1 cup grated Cheddar cheese

Wash spinach and cook in oil over high heat for 2 minutes. Toss with lemon juice, salt, and pepper. Line 2-quart casserole with spinach. Arrange lamb on top and cover with béchamel sauce combined with cheese. Brown in 400°F oven for 20 minutes.

Tourtiére (Pork Pie)

"A traditional French Canadian New Year's Day treat."
Nancy Albertini

Serves: 6 to 8
Bake: 40 to 60 minutes at 350°F

- 1 small onion, chopped
- 1 teaspoon sage
- 1½ pounds ground, lean pork
- ¼ cup water
- ½ teaspoon allspice (optional)
- 1 to 2 cups mashed potatoes
- Dough for 2-crust pie

Combine onion, sage, pork, water, and allspice and cook for 25 minutes. Cool. Add mashed potatoes and stir thoroughly. Line pie plate with ½ dough and fill with meat mixture. Cover with remaining dough, sealing well along sides. Bake at 350°F for 40 to 60 minutes.

Fruit-Stuffed Pork Crown Roast

"This recipe doubles nicely for a crowd."
Mrs. Robert G. Coseo

Serves: 8
Bake: 25 to 30 minutes per pound at 350°F

- 6 cups cubed, day-old bread
- 2 16-ounce cans apricot halves, chopped, reserve liquid
- 2 cups diced, peeled apples
- ½ cup chopped, cooked prunes
- 1 onion, chopped
- 1 cup chopped celery
- ½ cup butter, melted
- 1 teaspoon salt
- 1 teaspoon cinnamon
- ½ teaspoon ground cloves
- ½ teaspoon thyme
- 1 pork crown roast (16 ribs)
- Honey
- 1 cup water
- ½ cup sherry

Combine bread, fruit, onion, celery, butter, and seasonings. Add enough apricot liquid to moisten. Set aside. Place roast in baking pan and bake at 350°F for 25 to 30 minutes per pound, or until meat thermometer registers 170°F. About 1 hour before end of baking time, place stuffing in 2-quart casserole and bake in oven with meat. Baste roast with honey during last 20 minutes. Remove to heated platter and place stuffing in center of crown. Skim fat from baking pan. Add water to drippings and cook, stirring up brown particles. Add sherry and thicken if desired. Serve sauce with roast.

Pancet

"An authentic Korean dish—good for buffets."
Beverly Runge Willson

Serves: 6
Cook: about 40 minutes

- 1 cup water
- 3 pork chops
- 2 tablespoons cooking oil
- 2 cloves garlic, finely minced
- 3 medium yellow onions, thinly sliced
- ⅓ to ½ pound fresh green beans, thinly sliced on diagonal
- 4 tablespoons soy sauce
- 3 carrots, thinly sliced on diagonal
- 3 stalks celery, thinly sliced on diagonal
- 1 cup cabbage, coarsely cut
- 3 chicken bouillon cubes
- Dash Accent (optional)
- 8 ounces rice noodles
- Salt to taste

In covered pan, bring water to a boil and simmer chops until done, about 25 minutes. Save broth. Sliver meat into narrow pieces and discard bones and fat. In 5-quart pot, or wok, brown meat on high heat with cooking oil and garlic. Add onions and stir-fry until limp. Add beans, ¼ cup meat broth, and ½ soy sauce. Stir-fry 2 more minutes. Add carrots, celery, ¼ cup meat broth, and remaining soy sauce. Stir-fry. Add cabbage, bouillon cubes and Accent. Simmer about 4 minutes. Rinse rice noodles in warm to hot water until limp. Add to vegetable-meat mixture and toss. Add salt.

Pork Tenderloin with Apricot Sauce

"Always be sure to cook pork thoroughly."
Teresa Thomas

Serves: 2
Broil: 10 minutes

- 3 tablespoons apricot preserves
- Powdered ginger
- Freshly ground white pepper
- ½ teaspoon honey
- White wine
- 1 pork tenderloin, fat removed, cut in cross sections, and sliced ½- to ¾-inch thick
- 2 tablespoons heavy cream

Heat apricot preserves, adding spices and honey. Dilute with small amount of wine to glaze-like consistency. Place tenderloin in broiling pan and coat with preserves. Sprinkle with additional spices. Broil 5 minutes. Turn, and coat with more preserves. Broil 5 more minutes. Test for doneness. Place tenderloin in warmed serving dish. Drain pan drippings of fat and heat with white wine to degrease. Add cream to make sauce. Note: Watch broiler to prevent burning.

Chili Verde

"From a Mexican friend."
Mrs. Rex McCulloch

Serves: 4 to 6
Simmer: 1 to 2 hours

- 2 pounds lean pork shoulder, cut in ½-inch cubes
- 2 tablespoons flour
- 2 tablespoons shortening
- 1 cup chopped onion
- 4 large cloves garlic, finely minced
- 1 16-ounce can whole tomatoes, coarsely chopped
- 3 7-ounce cans diced green chilies
- ¼ teaspoon oregano
- 2½ teaspoons salt
- 2 cups water
- 2 tablespoons chili powder
- 1 tablespoon cilantro (optional)

Dredge meat in flour. Melt shortening in large deep skillet. Brown meat thoroughly. Add onion and garlic. Cook until onion is limp. Add remaining ingredients. Simmer covered for 1 to 2 hours, stirring occasionally. Remove cover and simmer until sauce is slightly thickened. Note: Serve with warm flour tortillas or over rice.

Spicy Sausage with Cabbage and Noodles

"A quick 30 minutes produces this hearty dish."
Terri Priest

Serves: 4

- 1 pound hot Italian sausage
- 1 small head (about 1 pound) Savoy or purple cabbage
- 2 tablespoons water
- 1 12-ounce package wide noodles
- Grated Romano cheese

Remove casing from sausages and brown thoroughly. Drain all but 2 tablespoons fat. Wash and shred cabbage, place over sausage, and add water. Simmer about 10 minutes, covered. In separate pan, cook noodles al dente. Drain well and add to sausage and cabbage mixture. Toss quickly and serve with grated Romano cheese.

Sweet-and-Sour Pork

"Serve with boiled rice."
The Cookbook Committee

Serves: 3 to 4
Cook: 15 minutes

- 1 egg
- 1 cup plus 1 tablespoon cornstarch
- 1 tablespoon water
- ¼ teaspoon baking soda
- 1 cup cubed pork butt
- 2 cups plus 1 tablespoon oil
- 2 bunches scallions, cut in 1-inch pieces
- 1 clove garlic, mashed
- 1 green pepper, cut in strips
- 1 tablespoon grated fresh ginger
- 1 20-ounce can pineapple chunks

Sauce

- 3½ tablespoons white vinegar
- ¾ teaspoon salt
- 2 tablespoons Worcestershire sauce
- 2 teaspoons cornstarch
- ½ teaspoon Accent
- 5 tablespoons sugar
- 2½ tablespoons cold water
- 4 tablespoons ketchup
- 1 teaspoon cooking sherry
- Red food coloring (optional)

Mix egg, 1 tablespoon cornstarch, water, and baking soda. Add pork and marinate for 15 minutes. Drain pork pieces and roll in remaining cornstarch. Heat 2 cups oil in frying pan until hot but not boiling. Add pork pieces 1 at a time and fry until golden brown. Drain on paper towels. In separate pan, heat remaining oil until hot. Add vegetables and stir-fry 3 minutes. Combine all sauce ingredients, add to vegetables, and bring to a boil. Add pork and pineapple and stir lightly. Reduce heat and keep warm until ready to serve.

Québec Ragôut de Boulettes

"Be generous with spices; test flavor often."
L. Paul Courchesne

Serves: 6 to 8
Simmer: about 30 minutes

- 1 pound lean ground pork
- 1 pound lean ground beef
- 1 medium onion, minced
- 2 tablespoons parsley, chopped
- ¼ teaspoon ginger
- ¼ teaspoon cinnamon
- ¼ teaspoon ground cloves
- ¼ teaspoon dry mustard
- 4 slices bread, cubed
- ½ cup milk
- Salt and pepper
- 3 tablespoons fat
- 5 cups water
- 5 tablespoons browned flour
- ½ cup Burgundy (optional)

Mix meat with onion, parsley, ginger, cinnamon, cloves, and mustard. Soak bread in milk, add to meat mixture and mix well. Add salt and pepper to taste. Shape into medium-sized meatballs. In Dutch oven, brown meatballs in fat, in batches if necessary. Add 4 cups water, cover, and simmer 30 minutes. Blend flour, remaining water, and wine until smooth. Pour over meatballs and continue simmering and stirring gently until gravy thickens. Serve with potatoes or rice. Crusty bread is a must.

Casserole Pork Chops

"Serve with cinnamon-flavored applesauce."
Mrs. Neal T. Skillings

Serves: 6
Bake: 2 hours at 325° to 350°F

- 2 large onions, thinly sliced
- 1 tablespoon sage
- 1 heaping tablespoon flour
- 1 teaspoon salt
- ½ teaspoon pepper
- 6 thick, loin pork chops, all fat removed
- 2 bouillon cubes, dissolved in 2 cups boiling water

Layer onions in bottom of 2-quart greased casserole. Mix sage, flour, salt, and pepper and dredge chops heavily. Place chops on onions and pour hot bouillon over. Cover and bake at 325° to 350°F for about 2 hours.

Jambalaya

"Great for leftover ham."
Kim Cutler

Serves: 4
Cook: about 35 minutes

- 3 onions, sliced
- 1 green pepper, cut in 1-inch strips
- 1 clove garlic, minced
- ½ cup butter
- ½ cup dry white wine
- 2 cups diced ham
- 1 18-ounce can tomatoes
- ½ teaspoon thyme
- ¼ teaspoon basil
- ¼ teaspoon paprika
- ½ teaspoon Tabasco
- 1 cup rice

Sauté onions, pepper, and garlic in butter for about 10 minutes. Add wine, ham, tomatoes, and seasonings. Mix well. Bring to a boil and add rice gradually, stirring constantly. Reduce heat, cover, and simmer 25 minutes or until rice is done. Note: Jambalaya is a creole dish and can be prepared with chicken, shrimp, ham, or a combination of all three.

Veal with Mushrooms and Cream

"The sour cream makes it very rich."
Diane Ryan Kunkler

Serves: 4
Cook: about 35 minutes

- Flour
- Salt and pepper
- 4 veal cutlets, pounded thin
- 1 tablespoon oil
- 4 tablespoons butter
- ½ cup chopped onion
- ½ pound mushrooms, sliced
- ¼ cup dry white wine
- ½ cup heavy cream
- ½ cup sour cream (optional)

Season flour with salt and pepper and dredge cutlets lightly. Sauté in oil and ½ butter until golden on each side. Remove to platter. Add remaining butter to pan and sauté onions and mushrooms until all liquid evaporates. Add wine and bring to a boil. Add cream and bring back to a boil. Return veal to skillet and simmer 20 minutes. Add more cream to skillet if necessary, but sauce should be thick. (Dish may be prepared in advance up to this point.) Stir in sour cream when ready to serve.

Hungarian Veal

"Better when reheated."
Helen Spool

Serves: 8
Bake: 2 to 3 hours at 350°F

- 2 tablespoons corn oil
- 4 cups sliced onion
- 4 pounds boneless veal roast (rolled leg or rump)
- 1 to 3 tablespoons Hungarian paprika
- 2 tablespoons finely chopped garlic
- Salt and pepper
- 2 tablespoons flour
- 2½ cups canned chicken broth
- 1 cup dry white wine
- 1½ cups sour cream at room temperature

Preheat oven to 350°F. Heat oil in Dutch oven and add onion. Add veal and cook until it loses red color, turning often. Sprinkle with paprika. Add garlic and salt and pepper to taste. Sprinkle meat with flour. Add chicken broth and wine. Bring to a boil. Cover and bake 2 to 3 hours. Baking time will depend on quality of veal. When meat is tender, add sour cream. Slice and serve over noodles.

Veal Scallop Paprika

"Serve with egg noodles."
Mary A. Pantano

Serves: 6
Cook: 5 minutes

- 1 to 1½ pounds veal cutlets, sliced thin
- Salt and white or freshly ground black pepper
- Hungarian paprika
- ½ cup grated Parmesan cheese
- ¼ cup plus 1 generous tablespoon flour
- ⅓ cup butter
- ½ cup water

Pound veal very thin and cut any white fibers with sharp knife. Spread flat. (You can halve to make scallops about 4 inches round.) Lightly sprinkle with salt, pepper, and paprika. Turn cutlet and sprinkle with paprika only. Mix Parmesan cheese with ¼ cup flour. Lightly cover veal with mixture. Shake off excess and let stand for a few minutes. Melt butter in large skillet, being careful not to burn. Sauté cutlets over high heat about 2½ minutes on each side. Remove to warm platter. Add remaining flour to pan and stir quickly to bind pan drippings. Add enough water to make smooth gravy. Stir until smooth and pour over veal. Serve immediately.

Risotto with Chicken and Veal

"Well worth the constant attention necessary."
Pat O'Brien

Serves: 6
Cook: about 30 minutes

- ⅓ cup olive oil
- ¼ pound veal, sliced for scallopine and cut in ½-inch cubes
- 1 pound chicken breasts, skinned, boned, and cut in 1½-inch cubes
- Salt and pepper
- 4 chicken livers, trimmed and cut in ½-inch cubes
- ¼ cup finely chopped onion
- ½ teaspoon finely minced garlic
- ½ teaspoon saffron
- 3 cups rice
- 2 cups dry white wine
- 7½ cups chicken broth
- ¼ cup butter
- 1 cup freshly grated Parmesan or Romano cheese

Heat oil in small casserole to almost smoking and sauté veal quickly, about 30 seconds. Add chicken breasts, salt, and pepper and sauté until slightly browned. Add liver and sauté, stirring, until it loses raw look. Add onion, garlic, and saffron and cook, stirring, about 1 minute. Add rice and stir to coat grains. Add wine and cook, stirring often, until absorbed. Add broth about 2 cups at a time and cook, stirring between each addition, until absorbed. Just before serving, stir in butter and cheese.

Lapin Italien

"A rich, peasant-style stew."
Mrs. Paul E. Reynolds

Serves: 4
Bake: about 2 hours at 300°F

- 1 medium rabbit, cut up (discard rib cage and liver)
- Flour (optional)
- 3 tablespoons olive oil
- 1 large green pepper, chopped
- 1 large onion, chopped
- 1 clove garlic, minced
- 4 medium tomatoes, peeled and cut in wedges
- 1 teaspoon salt
- ⅓ teaspoon pepper
- 1 teaspoon oregano
- Dry white wine

Rinse rabbit in cold water and dry with paper towels. Dredge in flour and brown in oil. In heavy Dutch oven, add remaining ingredients and just enough wine to simmer slowly on top of stove, or bake at 300°F for about 2 hours, until tender. Serve meat with sauce in pan over rice or pasta.

A Woman with Cows
Jean-François Millet
(French 1814–1875)
Pastel and charcoal on blue paper,
19.2 x 30.6 cm
Bequest of Mrs. Charlotte E. W.
Buffington, 1935.40

Cheese, Eggs, Pasta

Vegetarian Quiche Niçoise

"Best with fresh basil."
Patricia Leonard Bagg

Serves: 6 to 8
Bake: 50 minutes

- Pastry for 9- or 10-inch quiche pan
- 2 pounds Italian plum tomatoes, peeled and seeded
- 3 tablespoons olive oil
- 1 clove garlic, minced
- 1 teaspoon salt
- Pepper
- 2 tablespoons plus 1 teaspoon parsley, chopped
- 1 teaspoon dry basil, or 2 teaspoons fresh basil
- 1 pound onions, sliced
- 2 tablespoons butter
- ⅓ cup grated Parmesan cheese
- ½ pound mozzarella cheese, thinly sliced
- 3 eggs, beaten
- 1 cup cream
- 1 tomato, thinly sliced
- 6 olives, halved

Pre-bake pastry for 10 minutes at 425°F, then reduce heat to 375°F and bake 10 more minutes. Chop tomatoes, reserving juice. Heat olive oil in frying pan and cook garlic for a few minutes. Add tomatoes and juice, ½ teaspoon salt, pepper, and half the parsley and basil. Simmer until reduced by half, stirring occasionally. Sauce will be thick. In second frying pan, sauté onions in butter until golden. Stir in ¼ teaspoon salt. Sprinkle Parmesan over pastry. Spread onions over evenly. Cover with tomato sauce. Top with half the mozzarella. Mix together eggs, cream, and remaining salt and pour onto quiche. Add remaining mozzarella. Arrange tomatoes and olives alternately around top of quiche and sprinkle with remaining parsley and basil. Bake at 375°F for 30 minutes.

Zesty Baked Eggs

"Makes a nice brunch dish."
The Cookbook Committee

Serves: 4
Bake: 12 to 15 minutes at 350°F

- ⅓ cup mayonnaise
- ¼ teaspoon salt
- ⅛ teaspoon pepper
- ½ teaspoon paprika
- ½ teaspoon Worcestershire sauce
- ½ cup milk
- 1 cup grated sharp Cheddar cheese
- 8 eggs
- Ham, chopped, or a slice under eggs in ramekin (optional)

In saucepan, combine mayonnaise with seasonings. Gradually add milk while stirring. Add cheese and cook over low heat until cheese is melted. Pour 3 tablespoons sauce into each of 4 buttered ramekins. Add ham. Break 2 eggs into each ramekin and top with remaining sauce. Place ramekins in pan of hot water and bake 12 to 15 minutes at 350°F until eggs are done.

Sausage and Cheese Strata

"Prepare a day ahead for richer flavor."
Sarah Cederbaum Ribeiro

Serves: 4
Refrigerate: overnight
Bake: 1 hour at 350°F

- ½ pound sausage meat
- 1 medium onion, finely chopped
- 8 slices homemade-style white bread, crusts removed and cut in ½-inch cubes
- ¾ pound Monterey Jack cheese, grated
- 4 large eggs, lightly beaten
- 1½ cups milk
- ½ teaspoon salt
- 2 teaspoons Dijon mustard
- Pinch cayenne
- 1 teaspoon Worcestershire sauce

Brown sausage in skillet, breaking it up with fork. Drain on paper towels. Brush 1-quart soufflé dish with some of the fat. Sauté onions in remaining fat, then drain. Put one-third of bread cubes in bottom of dish and sprinkle with one-third of cheese. Arrange sausage over mixture, then sprinkle with onions. Add half the remaining crumbs and sprinkle with half the remaining cheese. Top mixture with remaining bread and press layers down slightly. Mix together eggs, milk, salt, mustard, cayenne, and Worcestershire sauce and pour over layers. Sprinkle with remaining cheese. Cover and refrigerate overnight. Let mixture stand at room temperature for 45 minutes and bake at 350°F for 1 hour, or until top is golden brown and filling is set.

Chili-Cheese Brunch

"Wonderful served with fresh fruit."
The Cookbook Committee

Serves: 8 to 10
Refrigerate: overnight
Bake: 45 minutes at 350°F

- ½ pound Swiss cheese, grated
- 1 pound Cheddar cheese, grated
- 6 eggs
- 2½ cups milk
- Salt and pepper
- 6 English muffins, split and quartered
- 2 4-ounce cans hot, green chilies

Combine Swiss and Cheddar cheeses. In separate bowl, combine eggs, milk, salt and pepper. Butter 9 x 15-inch pan and layer in following order: half of each ingredient —muffins, cheese, egg mixture, and chilies. Repeat. Make 1 day ahead and refrigerate. Bake at 350°F for 45 minutes.

Egg Soufflé

"Serve with bacon or sausage."
Celeste Thomaris Moschos

Serves: 6 to 8
Bake: 1 hour at 300°F

- 12 slices bread, crusts removed
- ¼ pound butter
- ½ pound Kraft Old English cheese
- 6 eggs
- 2 cups milk
- 1 teaspoon salt
- ¼ teaspoon dry mustard

Cube bread and put in 2½-quart casserole. In heavy pan, melt butter and cheese and pour over bread. Beat eggs well and add milk, salt, and dry mustard. Pour over bread and mix lightly. Refrigerate overnight. Remove 1 hour before baking. Place uncovered casserole in pan of water and bake at 300°F for 1 hour.

Spinach-Cheese Soufflé

"A nice custard texture."
Paula Connolly

Serves: 4
Bake: 1 hour at 350°F

- 1 pound cottage cheese
- 3 eggs
- 2 tablespoons butter
- 6 ounces sharp Cheddar cheese
- 1 10-ounce package frozen, chopped spinach, cooked and drained
- 3 tablespoons flour
- Salt to taste

Blend cottage cheese and eggs together. Cut butter and Cheddar cheese into small bits and add to egg mixture. Squeeze spinach dry and add to mixture. Stir in flour and salt. Place in 1-quart, greased casserole. Bake uncovered at 350°F for 1 hour, or until it is custard consistency and browned on top. Let settle 5 to 10 minutes before serving.

Easy Quiche

"I have to confess that it is better freshly made. I learned this the day the dog ate the one I made the day before, and I had to make a new one for lunch."
Polly Cowan

Serves: 6
Bake: about 1 hour

- 1 9-inch, frozen pie shell
- 4 ounces Swiss or sharp Cheddar cheese, coarsely grated or chopped
- 4 eggs, beaten
- ¼ cup milk
- 1 cup creamed cottage cheese
- Chives, chopped onion, or dried herbs to taste
- ½ teaspoon salt
- Pepper to taste

Let frozen crust thaw 10 to 15 minutes, or until slightly softened. Prick pie shell all over with fork, put another pie plate inside, and bake 10 minutes at 450°F. Remove from oven and cool. Sprinkle cheese over bottom of shell. Mix remaining ingredients thoroughly. Pour over cheese. Bake at 350°F for 45 to 50 minutes, or until silver knife comes out clean. Serve warm.

Havgitov Sbanakh

"Open-faced spinach-egg supreme."
Sona Husisian

Serves: 4

- 1 pound fresh spinach, washed and drained
- 3 medium onions, chopped
- 4 tablespoons olive oil
- ½ teaspoon salt
- ⅓ teaspoon pepper
- 4 teaspoons butter
- 4 eggs
- Paprika

Place spinach leaves in saucepan. Cover and cook 5 minutes over moderate heat. Drain thoroughly and chop coarsely. In skillet, sauté onions in oil until soft but not browned, stirring frequently. Add spinach, salt, and pepper. Mix well and cook about 10 minutes, or until liquid in pan has evaporated. In skillet, make 4 wells in spinach. Add 1 teaspoon butter to each well and break 1 egg into each. Cook over moderate heat, covered, until eggs are firm. Sprinkle with paprika. *Do not mix after adding eggs.*

Ham and Eggs, from *A Portfolio of Photographs by Ralph Steiner*
Ralph Steiner (American b. 1899)
Gelatin-silver print, 24 x 19 cm
Austin S. Garver Fund, 1978.106

Fettucine with Broccoli and Chicken

"Marco Polo would have loved this."
Joan D. Yood

Serves: 4 as main course
8 as first course

- 1 pound fettucine
- ½ cup sesame oil
- 1 cup boneless chicken breast, diced
- 2 teaspoons garlic, minced
- 2 teaspoons fresh ginger, slivered
- 3 cups packed broccoli flowerets
- ½ cup dry sherry
- ½ cup soy sauce
- 3 tablespoons butter
- ½ cup freshly grated Parmesan cheese
- ½ cup toasted almond slices

Cook fettucine in boiling, salted water according to package directions. While pasta is cooking, heat oil in wok or frying pan until smoking hot. Stir-fry chicken 1 minute, or until done. Add garlic, ginger root, and broccoli. Stir-fry 1 minute. Add sherry and soy sauce and simmer 1 minute. Drain fettucine. Rinse with cold water and toss with butter in chicken mixture. Add Parmesan and toss again. Garnish with toasted almonds.

Pasta with Vegetable Sauce

"No salt is added, so this is good for a low-sodium diet."
Sally Levinson

Serves: 6
Cook: 15 minutes

- ⅓ cup chopped onion
- 1 teaspoon minced garlic
- 2 tablespoons vegetable oil
- 1 pound zucchini, sliced ¼-inch thick
- ½ pound mushrooms, sliced
- ½ cup chopped green pepper
- ½ cup grated carrots
- 1 12-ounce can tomato sauce
- 6 ounces dry red wine
- 1½ teaspoons basil
- 1 teaspoon oregano
- ½ to ¾ pound linguine
- Parmesan cheese (optional)

In large skillet, sauté onion and garlic in oil for two minutes, stirring constantly. Add zucchini, mushrooms, green pepper, and carrots. Sauté 5 minutes, stirring frequently. Add tomato sauce, wine, basil, and oregano. Mix well and simmer 5 minutes more. Cook linguine according to package directions and drain. Arrange pasta on warm platter and top with vegetable sauce. Serve with Parmesan cheese.

Spaghetti all'Albertina

"Good with a full-bodied Chianti, Risena, or Barolo."
Doris B. Martin

Serves: 4
Cook: about 15 minutes

- ¼ pound bacon, diced
- ½ cup dry white wine
- 1 pound spaghetti
- 4 eggs
- Black pepper
- ¾ cup grated Parmesan cheese

In frying pan, sauté diced bacon until crisp. Add white wine. Let boil until alcohol evaporates and juices reduce to ½ cup. Cook spaghetti in boiling, salted water for 12 minutes. Beat eggs in serving bowl. Drain spaghetti, add to serving bowl, and mix well with eggs and pepper. (No salt needed as bacon is salty.) Sprinkle with bacon and Parmesan cheese and serve.

Pasta with Cream-of-Crabmeat Sauce

"Serve wtih a large green salad and white wine."
Abby Ann Lavoie

Serves: 4 to 6
Cook: about 20 minutes

- ⅓ cup unsalted butter
- 1 cup peeled Italian plum tomatoes
- 2 or 3 tablespoons chopped Italian parsley
- Dash Tabasco, or to taste
- ¼ cup all-purpose cream
- 2 tablespoons vodka
- 1 pound linguine, preferably fresh egg pasta
- 4 to 5 ounces cooked crabmeat, partly cut in chunks and partly flaked

Melt butter in saucepan. Add tomatoes and mash into butter. Add parsley and Tabasco and simmer 6 minutes. Stir in cream and simmer 3 minutes. Add vodka and simmer again until evaporated. Cook pasta al dente in salted water. Drain thoroughly. Add to saucepan along with crabmeat and stir and cook for 30 seconds. If you wish, serve with more chopped parsley.

Ziti Altre Formaggi

"A full meal served with a salad."
Edith F. Romano

Serves: 4 to 6
Bake: 15 to 20 minutes at 375°F

- 1 pound ziti
- 5 quarts boiling, salted water
- 3 tablespoons sweet butter, softened
- ½ cup shredded Swiss cheese
- ½ cup shredded Fontina cheese
- ½ cup shredded mozzarella cheese
- 1 cup heavy cream
- ½ cup grated Parmesan cheese
- ½ teaspoon nutmeg

Cook ziti in boiling water for about 8 minutes, until al dente. Do not overcook. Drain and rinse with cold water to stop further cooking. In large bowl, mix butter with ziti until it is well coated. Add Swiss, Fontina, and mozzarella cheeses and cream. Toss well and add half the Parmesan, still tossing. Place in buttered, 2-quart casserole and sprinkle with remaining Parmesan and nutmeg. Bake at 375°F for 15 to 20 minutes, or until top is golden brown.

Barley Puff

"Marvelous with poultry or any kind of roast."
Mrs. A. Abbott Coblentz

Serves: 8 to 10
Bake: 3 hours at 325°F

- 1 cup barley
- 1 large onion, diced
- 1 clove garlic, chopped
- ½ cup butter
- 3 cups chicken broth
- 1 pound mushrooms, quartered if large
- Sugar
- Salt and pepper to taste

Lightly brown barley with onions and garlic in butter. Do not let garlic burn. Place barley mixture in ovenproof, 2½-quart, covered casserole. Add remaining ingredients. Bake at 325°F for 3 hours, or until firm.

Cheese Sauce Lasagna

"A very different type of lasagna—mild, but good."
Helen Spool

Serves: 12
Bake: 20 minutes at 325°F

Tomato Sauce

- 1 large onion, finely chopped
- 1 clove garlic, minced
- 6 sprigs parsley, finely chopped
- ¼ cup olive oil
- 1 1-pound 12-ounce can tomatoes
- 1 4-ounce can tomato paste
- 2 bay leaves
- 1 teaspoon salt
- ¼ teaspoon pepper
- ½ cup water
- 1 pound ground beef

Cheese Sauce

- 1 small onion, finely chopped
- 4 tablespoons butter
- 3 tablespoons flour
- ¾ cup grated Parmesan cheese
- Dash salt
- 2 cups milk
- 2 egg yolks
- 1 pound lasagna noodles

To make tomato sauce, fry onion, garlic, and parsley in hot oil. Add tomatoes, tomato paste, bay leaves, salt, pepper, and water. Stir until well mixed. Add ground beef, breaking it up into little pieces. Cover and cook over low heat for 45 minutes. Sauce will not be thick. To make cheese sauce, sauté onion in melted butter for 2 minutes. Do not brown. Mix in flour until smooth. Add grated cheese and dash salt. Gradually add milk, cooking over low heat and stirring constantly until sauce is as thick as heavy cream. Beat egg yolks slightly in separate bowl and add a little hot cheese sauce, slowly to prevent curdling. Add remaining cheese sauce and cook over low heat for 10 minutes. Remove from heat. Cook pasta as directed. Drain. Preheat oven to 325°F. Grease bottom of large baking dish. Arrange layer of pasta on bottom. Then pour over enough tomato sauce to cover pasta and add some cheese sauce. Continue layering until ingredients are all used, finishing with layer of cheese sauce. Bake at 325°F for 20 minutes. Set under broiler until bubbly and golden.

Noodles Romano

"It's rich and delicious."
Nancy Marie Coghlin

Serves: 4
Cooking time: about 15 minutes

- ½ cup butter, softened
- 2 tablespoons parsley, finely chopped
- 1 teaspoon crushed basil
- 1 8-ounce package cream cheese, softened
- Dash pepper
- ⅔ cup boiling water
- 8 ounces fettucine noodles
- 1 large clove garlic, finely minced
- ¾ cup freshly shredded or grated Romano or Cheddar cheese

In saucepan, combine ¼ cup butter with parsley and basil. Blend in cream cheese and pepper. Stir in boiling water and blend well. Keep warm on stove. Cook noodles according to package directions, 8 to 10 minutes. Drain. Sauté garlic in remaining butter, 1 to 2 minutes. Pour over noodles. Toss lightly and quickly to coat. Sprinkle with ½ cup cheese. Toss well. Serve noodles on warm plate. Spoon warm cream cheese sauce over. Sprinkle with remaining cheese, tossing lightly to blend. Serve immediately.

Double Crust Pizza

"Heartier than the popular, one crust version."
Pat Juska

Serves: 4 to 5
Bake: 7 minutes at 450°F; 25 minutes at 400°F

Crust

- 1 cup lukewarm water
- 1 teaspoon sugar
- 1 teaspoon salt
- 2 tablespoons salad oil
- 1 package dry yeast
- 3 to 3½ cups unsifted flour

Sauce

- 1 6-ounce can tomato paste
- ½ cup water
- ½ teaspoon salt
- ¼ teaspoon sugar
- 1 teaspoon crushed oregano
- 1 clove garlic, crushed
- Dash pepper

Topping

- ½ pound mushrooms, washed, dried, and sliced
- 1 or 2 teaspoons butter
- 8 ounces mozzarella cheese, shredded
- ⅓ cup grated Parmesan cheese
- ½ teaspoon crushed red pepper (optional)
- 1 stick pepperoni, or hot or sweet Italian sausage, cooked and sliced
- 2 medium green peppers, sliced
- 2 medium onions, sliced

To prepare crust, put first 5 ingredients in bowl. Add 1 cup flour and beat for 2 minutes with electric beater. Gradually add balance of flour, stirring by hand until dough no longer sticks to side of bowl. Place dough on lightly floured board and knead for 5 minutes. Place in greased bowl, turning over to grease top. Cover and let rise in warm place until double in bulk, about 45 minutes.

Meanwhile, prepare sauce by combining tomato paste, water, and seasonings. Set aside. For topping, sauté mushrooms in butter. Set aside. Combine mozzarella, two-thirds of Parmesan, and red pepper.

When dough is double in bulk, punch down, halve, and let rest on lightly floured board for 2 or 3 minutes to relax gluten. Form into 2 balls. Roll out 1 to fit 12-inch-wide x 1-inch-deep pizza pan, leaving slight overhang. Place dough into ungreased pan and spread with pepperoni. Top with cheese mixture.

Roll out remaining dough to same size. Place over bottom crust, folding edges together and pinching to form standing rim. Bake near bottom of oven at 450°F for 7 minutes. Remove and add sauce, mushrooms, green pepper, onions, and remaining Parmesan. Return to oven and bake at 400°F for about 25 minutes, or until pizza is browned and set. If crust browns too quickly, cover with foil. Remove from oven and let stand 5 minutes before cutting.

Patzquaro, Mexico, 1964
Henri Cartier-Bresson
(French b. 1908)
Photograph, 34.8 x 23.3 cm
Eliza S. Paine Fund in memory of
William R. and Frances T. C. Paine,
1969.73

Savory Kugel

"Can be prepared ahead and frozen unbaked; next day, bake and serve immediately."
Arleen R. Danford

Serves: 10 to 12 (more as a side dish)
Bake: 30 minutes at 350°F

- 1 pound spinach noodles
- 1 onion, sliced
- Butter
- 1½ cups grated Cheddar cheese
- 1 clove garlic, mashed
- ½ teaspoon dry mustard
- 1 bunch broccoli, cooked and diced
- 1 pound cottage cheese
- ¼ cup butter, melted
- 1 teaspoon tarragon
- Pepper to taste
- ½ head cauliflower, steamed and diced
- ¼ pound mushrooms, sliced
- ½ cup sour cream

Cook noodles until tender and drain. Sauté onion in small amount of butter. Combine 1 cup Cheddar cheese with all other ingredients. Put in buttered, 9 x 13-inch baking dish. Top with remaining cheese. Bake at 350°F for about 30 minutes.

Walnut-Spinach Pasta

"The walnuts add an interesting texture."
The Cookbook Committee

Serves: 6

- 1 pound spaghetti
- 1 pound fresh spinach
- ¼ cup butter
- 1 medium onion, chopped
- 1 tablespoon fresh basil, chopped, or ½ teaspoon dried basil
- Dash fresh, grated nutmeg, or double dash powdered nutmeg
- ½ cup chopped walnuts
- Salt and pepper to taste

Cook spaghetti al dente according to package directions. Drain. Wash spinach and steam for 3 to 4 minutes in water that clings to leaves after washing. Cook only until wilted. Melt butter in small skillet and sauté onion until tender but not brown. Add basil, nutmeg, and walnuts. Toss with spaghetti and spinach. Season to taste. Serve immediately.

Orzo with Broccoli

"An unusual pasta stir-fry."
Sylvia Rothschild

Serves: 8

- 2 pounds broccoli (about 1 bunch) cut in pieces
- 2 large cloves garlic, halved
- 2 tablespoons olive oil
- 2 cups diced kielbasa
- 1 pound orzo
- ¼ cup butter
- 1 cup freshly grated Parmesan cheese

Cook broccoli until tender but crisp. Cook garlic in oil, stirring, for 5 minutes without browning. Remove garlic, add kielbasa, and cook for 5 minutes. Add broccoli and brown lightly. Cook orzo according to package directions. Add butter and toss, then add broccoli and kielbasa mixture and toss again. Add Parmesan and mix well. Turn onto platter and serve with additional Parmesan, if desired.

Noodle-Cheese Pudding (Kugel)

"Can be served as a side-dish or a dessert topped with sour cream."
Hilda B. Betten

Serves: at least 20
Bake: 2 hours at 350°F

- 6 eggs
- 1 pound cottage cheese
- ½ pound farmer's cheese
- 1 8-ounce package cream cheese
- 1 8-ounce package broad noodles, cooked according to directions
- 6 tablespoons butter, melted
- ½ cup sugar
- 1 cup sour cream
- 1 teaspoon vanilla
- 2 cups milk
- ½ teaspoon salt

Streussel Topping

- ½ cup brown sugar
- 2 tablespoons butter

Cream together eggs and cheeses. Add all other ingredients. Pour into 9 x 13-inch baking dish and bake at 350°F for 30 minutes.

To make topping, mix sugar and butter. Sprinkle on pudding and bake up to 1½ hours longer at 350°F. Serve warm.

Noodles in Pecan Crust

"A unique, rich side dish."
Mrs. A. Abbott Coblentz

Serves: 6 to 8
Bake: 1½ hours at 350°F

Crust

- ¼ cup butter, melted
- ½ cup firmly packed brown sugar
- 1 cup coarsely chopped pecans

Pudding

- 1 8-ounce package medium noodles, cooked and drained
- 2 tablespoons butter, melted
- 2 eggs, lightly beaten
- ¼ cup golden raisins
- 8 dried apricots, coarsely chopped
- 1 apple, peeled and thinly sliced
- ¼ cup sugar
- ¼ teaspoon cinnamon

Topping

- 2 tablespoons butter
- ¼ cup crushed corn flakes

Pour butter into 1½-quart casserole and sprinkle with mixture of sugar and pecans. Set aside. Toss warm noodles in butter. Combine remaining pudding ingredients and mix thoroughly. Refrigerate. To make topping, melt butter, add crushed corn flakes, and mix well. Pour pudding mixture onto pecan crust. Sprinkle with topping and bake 1½ hours at 350°F. Remove from oven and let sit 15 minutes. Turn out onto platter or serve in casserole.

Stuffed Shells Florentine

"Reminiscent of an Old World favorite."
Martha C. Piehler

Serves: 10 to 12
Bake: 30 minutes at 375°F

Tomato-Meat Sauce

- 1 pound ground beef
- 2 1-pound 12-ounce cans crushed tomatoes
- Oregano, basil, salt and pepper to taste
- 1 clove garlic, minced
- ¼ cup red wine
- ¼ cup chopped parsley

Shells and Filling

- 2 10-ounce packages frozen, chopped spinach
- 16 ounces ricotta cheese
- 1½ cups grated Parmesan cheese
- ¼ cup butter, softened
- 1 teaspoon salt
- ¼ teaspoon pepper
- Dash of nutmeg
- 1 12-ounce package shells, large enough for filling

Béchamel Sauce

- 3 cups light cream
- 1 bay leaf
- ⅓ cup butter
- ⅓ cup all-purpose flour
- 2 teaspoons chicken-broth granules
- 1 teaspoon salt
- ¼ teaspoon white pepper
- Dash nutmeg

Brown meat. Drain off all fat. Add tomatoes, seasonings, wine, and parsley. Bring to a boil. Reduce heat. Simmer 25 minutes.

Cook spinach until thawed, stirring often. Cover and simmer 3 minutes. Drain until dry. Combine spinach with ricotta, Parmesan, butter, salt, pepper, and nutmeg. Cook shells al dente according to package directions. Drain well and stuff with filling. Spread meat sauce on bottom of 9 x 13 x 2-inch pan and arrange shells on top.

Scald cream with bay leaf. Let stand 5 minutes. Remove bay leaf. Melt butter in medium-sized saucepan. Add flour and cook, stirring constantly until it bubbles. Stir in cream, chicken granules, salt, pepper, and nutmeg. Continue cooking and stirring until sauce thickens and bubbles, about 3 minutes. Pour over shells. Bake at 375°F for 30 minutes, or until bubbly. To serve, garnish with chopped parsley.

Linguine and Chicken Livers

"An unusual combination of flavors."
Barbara Rothstein

Serves: 4 to 6
Cook: about 15 minutes

- 2 tablespoons vegetable oil
- 2 tablespoons butter
- 2 large onions, sliced julienne
- 1½ pounds chicken livers, halved
- 1 teaspoon dry tarragon
- Freshly ground pepper to taste
- 2 tablespoons flour
- 2 cups chicken broth
- 2 to 3 tablespoons cognac
- 1 pound linguine, cooked al dente
- 1 tablespoon butter
- 2 tablespoons grated Parmesan cheese

In large frying pan, heat oil and butter on low. Add onions and sauté gently until wilted. Add livers and sauté. Turn occasionally until done. Add tarragon, pepper, and flour and mix well. Add chicken broth and stir until bubbling and thickened, 3 to 5 minutes. Add cognac. Heat through. Serve on hot linguine tossed with butter and grated cheese.

Still Life, 1849
Severin Roesen (American 1815–1872)
Oil on canvas, 56.4 x 68.9 cm
Museum purchase, 1981.343

Vegetables

Sardinian Tomatoes

"Attractive buffet dish."
Joan B. Dean

Serves: 4 to 6

- 2 tablespoons minced basil
- 1 tablespoon minced parsley
- 1 large clove garlic, chopped
- 5 tablespoons olive oil
- 1½ tablespoons red wine vinegar
- Salt and freshly ground black pepper
- 4 large, ripe tomatoes, sliced
- 1 pound mozzarella, thinly sliced
- 1 red onion, sliced into thin rings
- 1 2-ounce can flat anchovies, well drained
- Parsley
- Black olives

In blender or food processor, combine basil, parsley, garlic, oil, and vinegar. Season with pinch of salt and pepper and blend until smooth. Set aside. On platter, alternate tomatoes and cheese, overlapping slices. Spoon dressing over salad. Add dash of pepper, top with onion rings and anchovies, and garnish with parsley and olives.

Tomatoes Stuffed with Zucchini and Summer Squash

"Tasty and different—worth the effort."
Adelaide S. Bennett

Serves: 8
Cook: 15 to 25 minutes

- 1 pound zucchini and summer squash, grated
- 2 teaspoons salt
- 8 tomatoes
- 1 onion, chopped
- 1 clove garlic, minced
- 2 tablespoons olive oil
- 2 tablespoons butter
- 1 cup light cream
- ½ cup Parmesan cheese
- Salt and pepper to taste

Sprinkle squash with salt, toss, and let sit 30 minutes. Drain, transfer to tea towel, and squeeze. Cut off tops of tomatoes and remove seeds. Sprinkle with salt and pepper. Bake tomatoes cut side down at 325°F for 5 minutes. Sauté onion and garlic in oil and butter over medium-high heat until translucent. Add squash and cook, stirring for 2 minutes. Stir in cream, salt, and pepper. Cool until cream is absorbed and stir in Parmesan cheese. Mound mixture in tomatoes and sprinkle with additional Parmesan. Broil 5 inches from heat for 3 to 4 minutes until golden, or bake at 350°F for 20 to 25 minutes and omit first baking of tomato cups.

Cabbage and Tomatoes

"For cabbage lovers."
Mrs. Harry E. Goll

Serves: 8
Cook: 25 minutes

- 3 to 4 tablespoons butter, or olive oil
- 1 small onion, chopped
- 2 cups canned, crushed tomatoes
- 1 medium cabbage, finely shredded
- ¼ cup red wine
- Salt and pepper to taste
- 1 tablespoon sugar

In large skillet, melt butter. Add onions and tomatoes and cook until heated through. Add cabbage, blend, and cook over medium heat about 10 minutes, stirring occasionally. Add wine, salt, pepper, and sugar and cook 15 minutes more. Best served immediately.

Spaghetti Squash with Cheesy Herb Butter

"Zippy taste for a bland vegetable."
Ann D. Arthur

Serves: 4 to 6
Bake: 1 hour and 15 minutes at 350°F

- 4 pounds spaghetti squash
- ¼ pound butter, room temperature
- ¼ cup minced parsley
- ½ teaspoon Spice Islands herb seasoning (Italian)
- ¼ teaspoon garlic salt
- ¼ teaspoon freshly ground black pepper
- ⅓ cup grated Parmesan cheese

Bake whole squash at 350°F for about 1 hour, or until easily pierced with fork. Remove from oven and halve. Remove insides, which look like spaghetti, with fork. In separate bowl, mix remaining ingredients. Stir mixture into squash and pour into 2-quart casserole. Heat uncovered in oven for about 15 minutes, or until hot. Note: Freezes well.

Zucchini Boats

"Good low-calorie, vegetarian meal. Even my children love it."
Rebecca B. Crocker

Serves: 8
Bake: about 20 minutes at 350°F

- 4 large zucchini
- 2 quarts vegetables, chopped (onions, tomatoes, carrots, corn, summer squash, etc.)
- Seasonings to taste (thyme, basil, sage, salt, and pepper)
- 5 ounces grated Swiss cheese

Wash zucchini, split lengthwise, and cut ends off. Scoop out core, leaving enough for boats to retain substantial shape. Add core to vegetable combination if desired. In large, heavy pot, cook chopped vegetables on low heat until soft, about 25 to 30 minutes, stirring occasionally. (Do not add water.) Purée in food processor or blender. Return to pot and boil slowly, stirring frequently, until reduced by half. Mixture should be very thick. (Mixture is liable to splash as it is reducing. Place a cover over it askew to let steam out.) Add cheese. Fill zucchini halves and bake at 350°F until bubbly, about 20 minutes.

Approaching Storm, 1940
Grant Wood (American 1892–1942)
Lithograph, 30.2 x 22.5 cm
Gift of Frederick Rice, 1954.158

Zucchini Soufflé

"Tasty with a spicy tang."
Donna Wilhelmsen

Serves: 5 to 6
Bake: 50 minutes at 325°F

- 1 pound ground sausage
- 5 to 6 medium zucchini (2 pounds)
- ¾ cup grated Parmesan cheese
- ¾ cup bread crumbs
- 1 to 2 tablespoons chopped parsley
- ¼ teaspoon salt
- ¼ teaspoon pepper
- 4 eggs, separated
- 2 tablespoons water
- Paprika

Brown sausage and drain. Remove zucchini ends and cook in small amount of boiling water until tender but crisp, about 8 minutes. Cut 3 or 4 zucchini slices and set aside. Finely chop remaining zucchini. In large casserole, combine cheese, bread crumbs, sausage, chopped zucchini, parsley, salt, and pepper. Beat egg yolks with water until blended. Stir into sausage mixture. Beat egg whites to stiff peaks and fold into mixture. Sprinkle with paprika and top with zucchini slices. Bake uncovered at 325°F for 50 minutes, or until set. Note: May be frozen before baking.

Zucchini Tart

"Almost like a quiche."
Mrs. Frederic H. Mulligan

Serves: 6 to 8
Bake: 25 minutes at 350°F

- 3 cups thinly sliced, peeled zucchini
- 1 clove garlic, chopped
- ½ cup finely chopped onion
- 2 tablespoons chopped parsley
- 4 cups Bisquick
- ½ cup Parmesan cheese
- ½ cup sliced mozzarella cheese
- ½ teaspoon salt
- ½ teaspoon oregano
- ½ teaspoon seasoned salt
- 4 eggs, lightly beaten
- Dash pepper
- ¼ pound fresh mushrooms, chopped

Grease 10-inch round or 9 x 13-inch oblong pan. Combine all ingredients except mushrooms and stir. Pour into pan and bake 25 minutes at 350°F, or until golden on top. Arrange chopped mushrooms as garnish. Serve hot or at room temperature.

Oven-Crisped Eggplant

"A wonderful year-round treat."
Mrs. Jacques J. Burguet

Serves: 4
Bake: 20 minutes at 400°F

- ½ cup fine saltine crumbs
- ¼ teaspoon fine oregano
- ½ teaspoon paprika
- ½ teaspoon salt
- 1 egg
- 1 tablespoon water
- 2 small eggplants
- ½ cup melted butter

Mix first four ingredients. Beat egg with water. Peel eggplant, slice into ½-inch rounds, and, if desired, cut into strips. Dip eggplant into egg mixture and then into crumb mixture. Let stand at least 30 minutes "to set." In single layers, place on buttered baking sheet and drizzle with melted butter. Bake at 400°F for 20 minutes. Note: To remove bitterness, soak eggplant in cold, salted water for 30 minutes before preparing. Drain well and dry with paper towels.

Eggplant Casserole

"Easily reheated."
Diane Ryan Kunkler

Serves: 6
Bake: 20 to 30 minutes at 350°F

- 1 medium eggplant, peeled and cubed
- ½ cup chopped onion
- 2 tablespoons butter
- 2 tablespoons flour
- 1 cup milk
- 4 slices Old English cheese, grated
- 1 14½-ounce can stewed tomatoes
- ½ teaspoon salt
- Seasoned bread crumbs

Boil eggplant until tender and drain well. Sauté onion in butter until tender, but not brown. Add flour and cook over low heat 2 minutes. Slowly add milk and bring to a boil, stirring constantly. Remove from heat and cool for 1 minute. Stir in cheese and add tomatoes and eggplant. Season to taste. Pour into a greased, 1-quart casserole and cover with seasoned bread crumbs. Dot with butter. Bake at 350°F for 20 to 30 minutes until bubbly and brown on top.

Tangy Marinated Broccoli

"May be served as an hors d'oeuvre. Try the marinade over other vegetables or chicken."
Mrs. Sam Daniel, Jr.

Serves: 10 to 12
Marinate: overnight

- 3 bunches broccoli, uncooked
- 1 cup cider vinegar
- 1 tablespoon sugar
- 3 tablespoons fresh dill, or 1 tablespoon dried dill
- 1 teaspoon salt
- 1 clove garlic, mashed
- 1 teaspoon pepper
- 1½ cups vegetable oil
- Lemon slices (optional)

Remove stalks and leaves, then separate broccoli into flowerets and wash thoroughly. Drain and place in large, shallow container. Set aside. Combine vinegar, sugar, dill, salt, garlic, pepper, and oil. Mix well and pour over broccoli. Toss gently to coat. Chill at least 24 hours, tossing several times. Garnish with lemon slices. May be served in marinade or drained.

Summer Corn in Winter

"The secret of this recipe is the fresh summer corn."
Philip R. Morgan

Serves: 4 to 6

Summer

- 1 dozen ears of in-season corn-on-the-cob

Bring large kettle of water to a boil and cook corn for approximately 6 minutes, or to individual taste. Make sure corn is undercooked by several minutes. Remove, drain, and let cool slightly. Remove corn from cob with a knife and place equivalent of 4 to 6 ears in separate plastic bags and seal tightly. Put in freezer.

Winter

- 1 bag of corn
- Approximately ½ cup cream, or milk
- Approximately 2 table-spoons butter
- Salt (optional)
- Freshly ground pepper

Let corn thaw. Place cream in saucepan with corn and butter. Sprinkle with salt and pepper. Bring slowly to simmer or slow boil and cook approximately 5 minutes, stirring occasionally.

Corn Pudding

"Don't overcook."
Tom L. Freudenheim

Serves: 8 to 10
Bake: about 1 hour at 350°F

- 5 eggs
- 3 cups milk
- 4 to 6 tablespoons butter, melted
- ⅔ cup flour
- 2 teaspoons baking powder
- 3 teaspoons sugar
- 1 teaspoon salt
- 3 cups corn, frozen or fresh
- 1 green or red pepper, peeled and finely chopped (optional)
- ½ cup onion, finely chopped
- 2 to 4 cloves garlic, minced
- 2 shallots, finely chopped (optional)
- ¼ to ½ cup grated Parmesan cheese, or ¼ cup grated Swiss cheese

Blend eggs, milk, and butter. Sift together flour, baking powder, sugar, and salt. In separate bowl, mix together corn, green or red pepper, onion, garlic, shallots, and cheese. Add flour mixture to corn mixture. Add egg mixture and stir until thoroughly blended. Pour into greased 1½-quart casserole. Set in pan of water and bake, uncovered, at 350°F for about 1 hour, or until set.

Caramelized Onions

"Good with pork chops."
The Cookbook Committee

Yield: 1 cup

- ⅓ cup sugar
- 2 large onions, sliced and separated into rings, or chopped
- 2 tablespoons butter
- ½ teaspoon finely shredded orange peel

In heavy skillet, heat sugar on medium without stirring until it begins to melt. Heat and stir about 3 minutes more until golden brown. Add onions, butter, and orange peel. Continue cooking and stirring 7 to 8 minutes, or until onions are tender and glazed. Sauce should have consistency of corn syrup.

Gratin Dauphinois

"Ideal for company, for it may be prepared ahead."
Christina Callahan

Serves: 8
Bake: 1 hour at 400°F

- 2 pounds Idaho potatoes
- 2 cups milk
- 1½ cups heavy cream
- 1 large clove garlic, crushed
- ¾ teaspoon salt
- ½ teaspoon white pepper
- Butter
- ½ cup Swiss cheese, grated

Peel, wash, and dry potatoes. Slice ⅛-inch thick. Place in large, heavy saucepan. Add milk, cream, garlic, salt, and pepper. Bring to a boil, stirring to prevent scorching. Pour potato mixture into buttered, shallow baking dish. Sprinkle cheese over top. Bake 1 hour at 400°F. Reduce heat to 375°F if it browns too quickly. Allow dish to stand 15 to 20 minutes before serving.

Petits Pois à la Française

"A hearty way to serve peas."
Jeannette M. Bonneau

Serves: 6
Cook: 20 to 25 minutes

- 1 bunch scallions
- ⅔ cup beef broth
- 1 teaspoon sugar
- ¼ cup coarsely chopped ham (optional)
- 3 tablespoons butter
- Black pepper, coarsely ground
- 3 cups peas, cooked tender and drained, or 2 10-ounce packages frozen small peas
- 1 small head Boston lettuce, shredded
- Pinch parsley, or chervil

Wash scallions and cut off and discard green tops. Cut in 1-inch pieces. In pot, combine scallions, broth, sugar, ham, butter, and pepper. Cook until scallions are tender, about 20 minutes. At last minute, add peas and lettuce. Cook a few minutes until barely done. Sprinkle with parsley.

Swedish Baked Potatoes

"In Sweden they are often served as a party variation of the dinner potato."
Virginia C. Harding

Serves: 8 to 10
Bake: 1 hour at 450°F

- 8 to 10 medium potatoes
- 3 tablespoons butter, melted
- Salt
- Unseasoned bread crumbs
- 4 to 5 tablespoons grated cheese

Preheat oven to 450°F. Peel potatoes. Approximately every ¼ inch, slice each potato most of the way through, leaving bottom in one piece. (Hint: Put one potato at a time on a large serving spoon and slice. The concave spoon keeps the knife from cutting completely through potato.) Put potatoes into a 9-inch square, buttered baking dish. Brush with melted butter, sprinkle with salt, bread crumbs, and grated cheese. Bake uncovered at 450°F until done, about 1 hour. Serve from baking dish. Variation: Put thin slices of onion between potato slices.

Potato Pudding (Kugel)

"Freezes well."
Riva T. Grace

Serves: 10
Bake: 40 minutes at 400°F

- 5 large white potatoes, peeled and chopped
- 3 eggs
- ⅓ cup Matzo meal
- 1 teaspoon grated onion
- ½ cup vegetable shortening
- 1 teaspoon baking powder
- 1 teaspoon salt
- Dash pepper
- Dash cinnamon

In food processor or blender, blend all ingredients. Mixture will be slightly coarse. Put into 10 greased custard cups. Bake at 400°F for 40 minutes.

Escalloped Asparagus

"A side dish that can be turned into a main course."
Mrs. David J. Milliken

Serves: 6 to 8
Cook: 20 minutes

- 2 tablespoons butter
- 2 tablespoons flour
- 1 teaspoon salt
- ⅛ teaspoon pepper
- ⅛ teaspoon tarragon
- ⅛ teaspoon nutmeg
- 1½ cups milk
- ½ cup shredded Cheddar cheese
- 3 cups cooked asparagus, cut in 1-inch pieces
- 1 cup stale bread crumbs

Melt butter and blend in flour, salt, pepper, tarragon, and nutmeg. Stir in milk gradually. Cook over low heat, stirring constantly, until thickened. Mix in cheese and drained asparagus. In greased 1½-quart casserole, arrange alternate layers of asparagus and bread crumbs, ending with bread crumbs on top. Dot top with butter, then cover and bake at 350°F for 20 minutes. Note: Cubed, cooked chicken and sautéed mushrooms may be added for a one-dish meal.

Dziranov Bamya (Okra with Apricots)

"A good accompaniment to shish-kebab."
Sona Husisian

Serves: 4 to 6
Cook: about 50 minutes

- 1 10-ounce package frozen whole okra
- 3 medium onions, sliced
- 4 tablespoons olive or vegetable oil
- 1 8-ounce can tomato sauce
- 12 halves dried apricots
- 1 cup cold water
- ¼ teaspoon salt
- ⅛ teaspoon pepper

Defrost okra. Add to pan of boiling water and heat for 1 minute. Drain, add to pan of cold water, and drain again. In heavy, covered pan, sauté onions in oil over low heat, stirring frequently. Cook until soft, but not brown. Add okra, tomato sauce, apricots, cold water, salt, and pepper. *Do not stir* at any time. Apricots and okra will remain whole when cooked. Cover and cook on medium-low for about 30 minutes. Lower heat and cook 10 more minutes. Serve from pan or transfer to serving dish without mixing.

Apple Yams

"Good with poultry."
The Cookbook Committee

Serves: 6
Bake: 1 hour and 15 minutes at 350°F

- 1 2½-pound can yams, drained
- 4 tart apples, peeled and thinly sliced
- ¾ cup firmly packed brown sugar
- Cinnamon
- 1 stick butter, melted

Butter 1½-quart baking dish. Starting with yams, alternate layers of yams and apples, sprinkling each layer with cinnamon, brown sugar, and melted butter. Arrange layer of apples over top. Cover and bake 30 minutes at 350°F. Uncover and continue baking 45 minutes, or until nicely browned.

Vegetarian Curry

"Serve with bowls of condiments such as chutney, raisins, coconut, peanuts, green onions, and black olives."
Marilyn J. S. Goodman

Serves: 6 to 8
Cook: 30 to 40 minutes

- 1 tablespoon chili powder
- 2 teaspoons cumin seed
- 2 teaspoons turmeric
- 1 teaspoon coriander seeds
- 1 teaspoon cardamom
- 1 teaspoon cinnamon
- 1 teaspoon ginger
- 2 large onions, chopped
- 3 cloves garlic, chopped
- 3 to 4 tablespoons oil
- 1 cup water
- 2 cups diced apples
- 3 sweet potatoes, diced
- 2 tomatoes, peeled and chopped
- 1 teaspoon salt
- 1 cup yogurt, or sour cream
- Tabasco sauce, to taste (optional)
- 3 hard-boiled eggs, quartered (optional)
- 1 piece tofu, chopped in large squares (optional)

In blender, mix dry ingredients to make curry powder. In large, deep skillet or saucepan, sauté onions and garlic in oil until translucent. Add curry powder (3 to 4 tablespoons good, commercial powder may be substituted for homemade), water, apples, potatoes, tomatoes, and salt. Simmer 20 to 30 minutes. Add yogurt, Tabasco, eggs, and tofu and simmer 10 more minutes, or until curry thickens. Serve over kasha (buckwheat groats) or a good Indian rice like Bismati.

Escalloped Celery

"Delightfully crunchy."
Mrs. Francis A. Ives

Serves: 6 to 8
Bake: 25 minutes at 375°F

- ½ cup butter
- 2 cups sliced fresh mushrooms
- 5 cups coarsely sliced celery
- ¼ cup slivered, blanched almonds (optional)
- 1 8-ounce can water chestnuts, sliced
- 3 tablespoons flour
- ½ cup evaporated milk
- 1 cup chicken broth
- ½ cup dry bread crumbs
- ½ cup Parmesan cheese

In skillet, melt 3 tablespoons butter. Add mushrooms and cook until tender. Set aside. Boil celery for 5 minutes and drain. Mix celery with almonds, water chestnuts, and mushrooms. Set aside. Melt remaining butter. Stir in flour and cook until it bubbles. Gradually add evaporated milk and chicken broth over low heat. Cook until thick and smooth, stirring constantly. Blend celery mixture into sauce and pour into buttered 1½-quart casserole. Just before baking, top with bread crumbs and cheese. Bake at 375°F until hot and bubbly, about 25 minutes.

"New" Peas

"A new look for an old flavor."
Polly Cowan

Cook as many packages of frozen peas as you need for your guests. When done, purée in food processor, add butter to taste, and serve.

Pea Pods with Mushrooms

"Fresh and crisp."
Peter Levine

Serves: 4
Sauté: about 5 minutes

- 1½ tablespoons butter
- ¾ pound fresh, de-veined pea pods
- ⅓ pound fresh mushrooms, sliced
- 1 teaspoon soy sauce
- 1 teaspoon Worcestershire sauce

In frying pan, melt butter. Add pea pods, mushrooms, soy sauce, and Worcestershire sauce. Sauté over medium-high heat, approximately 5 minutes. Do not overcook.

Mushrooms Newburg

"Good as a luncheon or supper dish."
Vera Dowden Baldwin

Serves: 6
Bake: 20 minutes at 350°F

- 1 pound whole, fresh mushrooms
- ¼ cup melted butter, and 6 tablespoons butter
- 6 tablespoons flour
- 1½ cups chicken broth
- 1 cup light cream
- ½ cup white wine
- ½ cup sherry
- Salt and pepper to taste
- ½ cup slivered almonds

Wash and drain mushrooms. Simmer 10 minutes in small amount salted water and drain. Slice mushrooms and toss with melted butter. To make cream sauce, melt butter in saucepan. Stir in flour and cook 2 minutes. Do not let brown. Slowly add broth, cream, and wine. Cook and stir until smooth and thickened. Season with salt and pepper. Stir in sherry. Pour layer of sauce into 1½-quart casserole. Add layer of mushrooms and top with a few almonds. Repeat layers, ending with cream sauce and sprinkling of almonds. Bake at 350°F for 20 minutes.

Mushroom Casserole

"My most favorite of all mushroom recipes."
Mrs. Edwin G. Bagley

Serves: 8
Bake: about 40 minutes at 350°F

- 1½ pounds mushrooms, chopped
- ½ cup butter
- 4 tablespoons flour
- 1 cup light cream
- 3 eggs, separated
- Salt and white pepper

Sauté mushrooms in ¼ cup butter until tender. Drain, saving juices, and set aside. Melt remaining butter and whisk in flour. Slowly stir in cream and 1 cup of reserved juices. Heat until thickened, then cool. Add 1 cup sauce to sautéed mushrooms. Beat egg yolks and add to mushroom mixture. Add salt and pepper to taste. Beat egg whites until stiff and fold into mushroom mixture. Bake at 350°F in buttered casserole, placed in pan of water, for 40 minutes, or until set. Note: Leftover mushroom sauce makes good base for soup.

Carrot-Mushroom Stir-Fry

"Very nice color."
Arleen R. Danford

Serves: 4 to 6
Cook: 10 minutes

- 2 tablespoons butter
- 2 tablespoons corn oil
- 1 pound carrots, pared and thinly sliced
- ¾ pound mushrooms, thinly sliced
- 5 green onions with tops, thinly sliced
- 1 tablespoon lemon juice
- ¼ teaspoon salt
- ¼ teaspoon freshly ground pepper

In large skillet, heat butter and oil until bubbly. Add carrots, mushrooms, and onions. Cook and stir until vegetables are tender but crisp, about 5 minutes. Stir in lemon juice, salt, and pepper.

Mushroom Mania

"May be served on toast points, in large mushroom caps, or in zucchini halves."
Rosalie Olds

Serves: 8 to 10

- 2 pounds fresh mushrooms
- 4 tablespoons butter
- 4 tablespoons dry sherry
- 2 cups sour cream
- 1 cup Parmesan cheese
- ¼ cup soy sauce
- ½ teaspoon black pepper

Clean and slice mushrooms and sauté in butter. Add sherry and cook 1 minute. Blend in remaining ingredients and simmer until thickened.

Carrot Fondue

"Doubles easily."
Susan Dunlop Roberts

Serves: 4 to 6
Bake: 25 minutes at 350°F

- 1 pound carrots
- 4 tablespoons butter
- 1 green pepper
- 1 tablespoon chopped parsley
- 1 small onion, minced
- 2 tablespoons flour
- 1 cup milk, or part milk and part cream
- Salt and pepper
- 2 eggs, lightly beaten
- Bread crumbs

Cook, drain, and purée carrots in food processor or blender. In 2 tablespoons butter, brown green pepper, parsley, and onion. To make cream sauce, melt remaining butter in small, heavy pan. Stir in flour and blend well over low heat. Slowly stir in milk. Stirring constantly, bring slowly to a boil. Cook 2 minutes. Season with salt and pepper. Mix cream sauce with puréed carrots. Add pepper, parsley, onion, and beaten eggs. Place in ½-quart casserole, pat bread crumbs on top, and bake at 350°F for 25 minutes.

Peach-Glazed Carrots

"May be prepared ahead."
Mrs. Kalman S. Sinofsky

Serves: 6
Cook: 25 to 30 minutes

- 1½ pounds carrots
- ½ cup peach preserves
- 1 tablespoon butter, melted

Pare and slice carrots ¼-inch thick. Cook in salted water until tender. Drain. Arrange in skillet or large saucepan. Combine preserves and butter. Spoon over carrots. Heat on low about 15 minutes, or until hot.

Marinated Carrots

"Good for a summer buffet or cookout; better prepared ahead of time."
Martha Coe Varnum

Serves: 8
Cook: about 10 minutes

- 2 pounds carrots
- 1 small green pepper, finely chopped
- 1 small onion, finely chopped
- 1 10½-ounce can tomato soup
- ½ cup oil
- ½ cup sugar
- ¾ cup cider vinegar
- 1 teaspoon dry mustard
- 1 teaspoon Worcestershire sauce
- Salt and pepper

Cut carrots diagonally and boil until tender. Arrange layers of carrots, pepper, and onion in deep bowl. Combine remaining ingredients and pour over vegetables. Some liquid may be drained before serving.

Zesty Carrots

"Nice for covered-dish suppers."
Jeanette A. Henderson

Serves: 8 to 10
Bake: 30 minutes at 350°F

- 2 pounds carrots, diced and cooked
- 1 cup mayonnaise
- 2 tablespoons horseradish
- 6 tablespoons diced onion
- Bread crumbs

Toss together carrots, mayonnaise, horseradish, and onion and place mixture in casserole. Dust top with bread crumbs. Bake at 350°F for 30 minutes.

Carrots in Marsala

"Wonderful with chicken."
The Cookbook Committee

Serves: 6
Cook: about 10 minutes

- 1 pound fresh carrots
- 1 tablespoon butter
- ¼ cup Marsala
- 1 teaspoon salt
- ⅛ teaspoon pepper
- ½ cup water
- 1 tablespoon chopped parsley

Wash, pare, and cut carrots into thin, 2-inch strips. In large saucepan, combine carrots, butter, wine, salt, pepper, and water. Cover and bring to a boil. Reduce heat and simmer 10 minutes, or until almost tender. Uncover and simmer until most of liquid evaporates. Sprinkle with parsley.

Summer Vegetables

"Easy, colorful, and appealing."
Gale Y. Morgan

Serves: 6
Bake: 30 minutes at 450°F

- 2 large green peppers, thinly sliced
- 1 sweet pepper, thinly sliced
- 3 medium zucchini, and/or summer squash, sliced
- 1 medium eggplant, quartered and sliced
- 3 large onions, sliced (use regular and Bermuda onions)
- ⅔ cup olive oil
- Salt and pepper
- 1 to 2 cloves garlic, crushed

Lightly oil shallow baking dish and arrange vegetables in rows. Mix remaining olive oil with salt, pepper, and garlic and sprinkle over vegetables. Bake at 450°F for 30 minutes. Note: If serving cold, you may want to sprinkle with vinegar.

New England August Dinner

"A nice way to use your garden riches."
Beverly Runge Willson

Serves: 4 to 6
Bake: 1½ hours at 300°F

- 3 large potatoes, peeled and sliced in ¾-inch rounds
- 1½ pounds zucchini squash, cut in 1-inch rounds
- 3 to 4 large, ripe tomatoes, peeled
- 1 cup bread crumbs
- 1 clove garlic, chopped
- ⅓ cup freshly grated Parmesan cheese
- ⅓ cup olive oil
- Salt and pepper

Lightly grease a 3-inch-deep casserole. Arrange potato slices on bottom of dish and season. Add 1 layer zucchini slices and season. Halve tomatoes crosswise. Gently squeeze tomato juice over vegetables in dish and arrange tomato solids, cut side up, on top of vegetables. Combine breadcrumbs, garlic, cheese, and olive oil. Spread over top. Cover and bake 1½ hours at 300°F. Remove cover during last 30 minutes if crisp top is desired. Serve with red wine and loaf of Italian bread.

Turnip Casserole

"Even people who don't like turnips like this."
Les Hatch

Serves: 8
Bake: 30 to 40 minutes at 350°F

- 1 medium yellow turnip, cooked and mashed
- 1 teaspoon salt
- 2 tablespoons sugar
- ½ teaspoon cinnamon
- 2 tablespoons butter
- 4 tablespoons flour
- 2 eggs, well beaten
- ½ cup milk

Combine ingredients in above order. Beat well. Pour into greased casserole. Sprinkle top with additional sugar and cinnamon and dot with butter. Bake uncovered at 350°F for 30 to 40 minutes. Recipe may be halved or doubled.

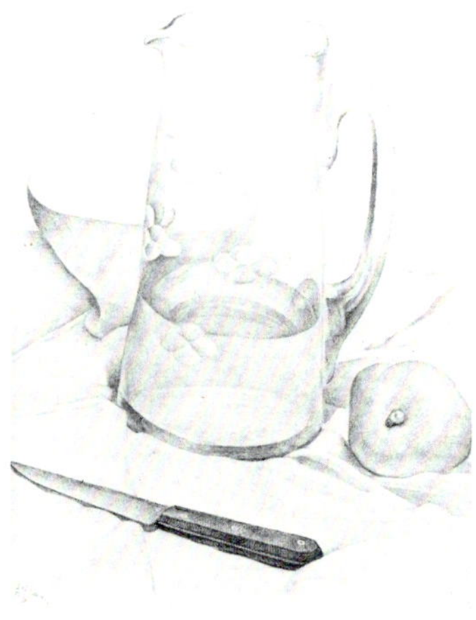

Water Pitcher, 1918
Diego Rivera (Mexican 1886–1957)
Graphite, 35.6 x 24.8 cm
Museum purchase, 1928.5

Spinach and Artichoke Casserole

"An unusual combination for a do-ahead dish."
Nancy Laird

Serves: 10
Bake: 30 minutes at 350°F

- 2 tablespoons butter
- 2 cups sliced mushrooms
- 1 14-ounce can artichoke hearts, halved
- 2 10-ounce packages frozen spinach, cooked and drained
- 1 10-ounce can cream-of-mushroom soup
- ¼ teaspoon garlic salt
- ½ cup sour cream
- ½ cup mayonnaise
- ½ teaspoon lemon juice

In frying pan, melt butter and sauté mushrooms 3 to 5 minutes until tender. Drain artichokes and place in a flat casserole. Combine spinach, soup, garlic salt, and mushrooms. Spread over artichokes. Combine sour cream, mayonnaise, and lemon juice. Spread over spinach mixture. Bake at 350°F for 30 minutes. If top needs browning, place under broiler.

Spinach Purée I

"Nice creamy texture."
Diane Ryan Kunkler

Serves: 4
Cook: about 5 minutes

- 2 10-ounce packages frozen chopped spinach
- ½ teaspoon salt
- 2 3-ounce packages cream cheese, room temperature
- 1 tablespoon chives, chopped
- 1 clove garlic, mashed

Cook spinach until just defrosted. Drain. In food processor or blender, combine spinach with remaining ingredients. Reheat before serving.

Spinach Purée II

"Try other fruits."
Mildred J. Riley

Serves: 4 to 5
Bake: 15 minutes at 350°F

- 2 packages fresh spinach, or 2 10-ounce packages frozen spinach
- 2 very ripe pears
- ¼ cup nonfat milk powder
- Salt and pepper

Cook spinach and drain well. Pare, core, and slice pears. Purée in food processor or blender until smooth. Add spinach and milk powder and mix until blended and smooth. Add salt and pepper to taste. Continue to process until spinach is very light and airy. Turn into baking dish and cover. Bake at 350°F for 15 minutes.

Radishes
Don Nice (American b. 1932)
Color lithograph, 96.5 x 68.6 cm
Museum purchase, 1977.71

Salads

♣

Antipasto Mastroianni

"A family recipe enjoyed for over 40 years. Makes a nice condiment with meat."
Mary K. Mastroianni

Yield: 13 pints
Cook: about 2 hours

- 1 medium head cauliflower
- 1 pound small onions
- 1 pound string beans
- 1 bunch carrots
- 1 pound red peppers
- 1 pound green peppers
- 1 bunch celery
- 3 pounds mushrooms (wild, if desired)
- ¼ cup butter
- 1 2-pound can anchovies
- 3 tablespoons sugar
- 3 tablespoons flour
- 2 6-ounce cans tomato paste
- 1 quart white vinegar
- 1 pint Italian olive oil
- 1 3¼-ounce jar capers
- 1 pint sour pickles, cut up
- 1 quart stuffed olives
- 1 13-ounce can tuna fish, drained and cup up

Cut vegetables into bite-sized pieces. Put in separate bowls and sprinkle with salt. Let stand overnight. In saucepan, boil each vegetable separately as follows: start first vegetable in ½ cup water, boil until tender, and remove with slotted spoon. Bring water up to ½ cup, and repeat with each vegetable. After cooking all vegetables, reserve liquid. Wipe mushrooms and quarter large ones, leaving buttons whole. In skillet, melt butter and sauté mushrooms a few minutes. Do not brown. In bowl, combine anchovies, sugar, flour, and tomato paste. In large, heavy kettle, boil white vinegar and olive oil for 10 minutes. Add vegetable water and anchovy-tomato paste. Stir over low heat until slightly thickened. Bring to a boil and add mushrooms, capers, pickles, olives, and vegetables. Boil 5 minutes, stirring constantly. Add tuna fish. Boil 5 minutes longer stirring constantly. Put in sterile jars and seal. Keeps up to 1 year in cool spot.

♣

Overnight Layered Salad

"Easy for parties."
Mrs. Richard B. Kennedy

Serves: 6 to 8
Refrigerate: overnight

- Lettuce
- 1 8-ounce can water chestnuts, sliced
- 1 large onion, sliced
- 2 to 3 sticks celery, sliced
- 1 10-ounce package frozen peas, uncooked
- 1 cup or more mayonnaise
- Parmesan cheese
- Cherry tomatoes
- Parsley
- Chives

Fill salad bowl half full of lettuce and layer water chestnuts, onion, celery, and peas. Frost top of salad with mayonnaise. Sprinkle with Parmesan. Cover and refrigerate overnight. Before serving, add tomatoes, parsley, and chives and toss.

♣

Salad Chez Blaine

"Good served after a rich meal."
Gaye Brown

Serves: 4 to 6

- 1 head Boston or red leaf lettuce
- 1 tablespoon butter
- ¼ cup chopped almonds
- 1 11-ounce can mandarin orange slices, chilled

Vinaigrette Dressing

- 5 tablespoons olive oil
- 2 tablespoons white vinegar
- ¼ teaspoon dry mustard
- ½ teaspoon salt
- ⅛ teaspoon pepper
- 1 clove garlic, halved

Wash lettuce, shake off excess water, and wrap in paper towels. Refrigerate until ready to serve. Melt butter in small fry pan and sauté almonds until toasted. Make sure almonds, not just butter, are browned. To prepare dressing, mix all ingredients in cruet and shake well. Arrange lettuce on salad plates. Drain orange slices and arrange on lettuce. Sprinkle with almonds and dressing and serve. Note: Keep dressing at room temperature.

♣

Cucumbers and Sour Cream

"Everyone liked it."
Mary Atamian

Serves: 6

- 4 cucumbers
- Salt to taste
- 2 or 3 medium onions, sliced long
- 2 pints sour cream
- 1 teaspoon vinegar
- 2 tablespoons sugar
- Garlic (optional)
- Parsley, or chives

Peel and slice cucumbers very thin. Place cucumbers, salt, and onions in bowl and cover with cold water. Let stand for 2 hours in refrigerator, then drain. Add sour cream, vinegar, sugar, and garlic. Refrigerate until ready to serve. Garnish with parsley or chives.

♣

Shanghai Salad

"Very versatile."
Ann D. Arthur

Serves: 10 to 12

- 1 pound bean sprouts
- 1 10-ounce can water chestnuts, thinly sliced
- ¾ cup slivered toasted almonds
- 2 to 3 quarts salad greens, washed and chilled

Herb Dressing

- 1⅔ cups mayonnaise
- 1 teaspoon prepared mustard
- ½ teaspoon Tabasco
- 1 tablespoon chili sauce
- ½ teaspoon onion salt
- 1 teaspoon chili powder
- ⅛ teaspoon garlic powder
- 2 tablespoons vinegar
- 1½ teaspoons marjoram
- ¾ teaspoon thyme

Toss together sprouts, water chestnuts, almonds, and salad greens. In separate bowl, blend dressing ingredients vigorously, adjusting flavor with more onion and/or garlic. Mix desired amount of dressing with salad and refrigerate. Serve cold. Variations: Add chicken, turkey, ham, cheese, or seafood.

♣

Fairmont Mustard Ring

"Nice mustard bite."
Julie Chase Fuller

Serves: 8
Refrigerate: 1½ hours

- 4 eggs
- ½ cup sugar
- 1 tablespoon gelatin
- 1½ tablespoons dry mustard
- ½ teaspoon turmeric
- ¼ teaspoon salt
- 1 cup water
- ½ cup cider vinegar
- ½ cup whipping cream

Beat eggs in top of double boiler. In bowl, mix sugar and gelatin together thoroughly. Stir in mustard, turmeric, and salt. Add water and vinegar to eggs. Stir in sugar mixture. Cook over boiling water until slightly thickened, stirring constantly. Cool until thickened, about 1 hour. Fold in whipped cream that has been beaten to soft peaks. Pour into 1½-quart ring mold and refrigerate about 30 minutes. Unmold when ready to serve. Note: Center may be filled with black olives, cole slaw, or cooked baby shrimp.

♣

Two Week Salad

"A variation on coleslaw."
Frank T. MacGrory

Serves: 10

- 1 large cabbage
- 1 large onion
- ¾ cup vinegar
- ¾ cup vegetable oil
- 1 teaspoon salt
- 1 cup sugar

Chop the cabbage and onion coarsely. Place in bowl and mix. Boil together vinegar, oil, salt, and sugar. Pour hot dressing over vegetables and let stand 1½ hours before mixing. Store in covered container at least 12 hours before serving. Note: Salad may be prepared well in advance and kept refrigerated for up to two weeks.

Avocado and Mushroom Salad

"Refreshing."
Rebecca B. Crocker

Serves: 4

- 2 ripe avocados, peeled and diced
- ½ pound mushrooms, cleaned and sliced
- Italian dressing

Combine avocados with mushrooms and toss with dressing.

Sardine Salad

"Good as summer luncheon dish or an hors d'oeuvre."
Mrs. Israel S. Morin

Serves: 4

- 1 15-ounce can sardines in tomato sauce
- ½ cup elbow macaroni (or other pasta), cooked, drained, and cooled
- ½ cup chopped red onion
- Mayonnaise
- Lettuce

Drain sardines and reserve sauce. Bone and chop sardines, then toss with half of sauce, macaroni, onion, and mayonnaise to taste. Chill. Serve on lettuce leaves and decorate with scored cucumber slices, tomato wedges, or hard-boiled egg wedges. Variations: Make without tomato sauce, or add hard-boiled egg and use only ¼ cup macaroni.

Marinated Cabbage

"New twist for an old favorite."
Maureen A. Irish

Serves: 12 to 16
Refrigerate: 24 hours

- 1 small head cabbage, shredded
- 1 small onion, chopped
- 1 4-ounce jar pimento, chopped
- 1 cup cider vinegar
- ½ cup sugar
- ¼ cup oil
- 1 teaspoon prepared mustard
- 1 teaspoon celery seed
- 1 teaspoon salt
- ¼ teaspoon pepper

In large bowl, combine cabbage, onion, and pimento. Mix together vinegar, sugar, oil, mustard, celery seed, salt, and pepper. Pour over cabbage mixture. Cover and chill at least 24 hours. Will keep 3 to 4 days.

The Natural Salad

"I have made it several times and never found anyone who did not ask for the recipe."
Mary K. Hicks

Serves: 10 to 12

- 1 cup finely grated carrots
- 1 cup whole-wheat bread crumbs or cubes
- 1 cup grated sharp Cheddar cheese
- ½ cup sunflower seeds
- 1 cup diced celery
- 1 cup chopped parsley
- ½ cup raisins (optional)
- 1 cup diced onions (optional)
- 1 cup alfalfa sprouts (optional)
- Romaine lettuce

Dressing

- ½ cup oil
- 1 tablespoon Tamari
- 1 tablespoon honey
- 2 tablespoons lemon juice
- 2 teaspoons basil
- 1 teaspoon sage
- 1 teaspoon kelp (optional)

Combine all salad ingredients except lettuce. In separate bowl, combine dressing ingredients and stir. Add to first mixture and chill. Serve on or roll in Romaine. Good filling for Syrian bread.

Crunchy Pea Salad

"Add chicken to make a meal."
Sarah Cederbaum Ribeiro

Serves: 10

- 2 10-ounce packages frozen petite peas, thawed
- 1 cup chopped celery
- ¼ cup chopped green onion with 3 to 4 inches green tops
- 1 cup chopped cashews, or macadamia nuts
- ½ cup crisp bacon bits
- 1 cup sour cream
- ½ teaspoon salt
- ¼ cup Garden Café Dressing

Garden Café Dressing

Yield: 1 pint

- ⅓ tablespoon lemon juice
- ½ cup red wine vinegar
- ½ tablespoon salt
- ½ teaspoon finely ground pepper
- ½ tablespoon Worcestershire sauce
- ½ teaspoon Dijon mustard
- 1 clove garlic, mashed
- ½ teaspoon sugar
- 1½ cups corn oil

Combine peas, celery, onion, nuts, and bacon.

To make dressing, combine all ingredients except oil in blender or food processor. While processing, gradually add oil. Mix together sour cream and dressing and fold gently into pea mixture. Chill and serve on a bed of lettuce.

♣

Chili-Spiced Bean Salad

"Spicy hot."
Karson Y. Aubuchon

Serves: 8 to 10
Refrigerate: at least 6 hours

- 1 16-ounce can each red kidney, pinto, and garbanzo beans
- 1 16-ounce can whole-kernel corn
- ½ cup thinly sliced green onion
- ¼ cup chopped parsley
- 1 cup sliced celery
- 1 4-ounce can diced green chilies

Chili Dressing

- ¾ cup olive oil
- ¼ cup wine vinegar
- 1 clove garlic, minced
- 1½ teaspoons salt
- 1 teaspoon chili powder
- 1 teaspoon oregano
- ¼ teaspoon ground cumin
- ⅛ teaspoon liquid hot pepper seasoning

Place beans and corn in large colander. Rinse with water and drain well. In 4-quart salad bowl, combine bean mixture, green onion, parsley, celery, and chilies.

In small bowl or jar with cover, combine dressing ingredients. Stir or shake to blend thoroughly. Pour over salad, stirring to coat evenly. Cover and chill, stirring several times, for 6 hours or overnight.

♣

Slaw Salad

"An alternative to cole slaw."
Mrs. Kalman S. Sinofsky

Serves: 6 to 8
Refrigerate: 24 hours

- 1 medium head cabbage
- 1 large onion
- 1 medium green pepper, seeds removed
- 6 radishes
- 2 large cucumbers, not pared
- 3 carrots, pared
- ½ cup white vinegar
- ¼ cup vegetable or corn oil
- 2 teaspoons salt
- ½ cup sugar
- ¼ cup water
- Seasoned salt to taste

Remove and discard outer, loose cabbage leaves. Wash vegetables and let dry. Using slicing disc of food processor, slice cabbage, onion, pepper, and radishes. Thinly slice cucumbers into rounds. Using grating disc, grate carrots. Place vegetables in large, covered, airtight container. Mix remaining ingredients. Pour over vegetables. Refrigerate for at least 24 hours. Turn container or mix occasionally. Serve cold as side dish. Note: During marinating, vegetable volume decreases, liquid increases. Adjust seasonings.

♣

Russian Beet Mold

"Easily doubled."
Kim Cutler

Serves: 8 to 10
Refrigerate

- 1 16-ounce can julienne beets
- 1 envelope gelatin
- ⅓ cup wine vinegar
- 3 tablespoons sugar
- ½ small onion, grated
- ½ teaspoon seasoned salt
- Dash Tabasco

Horseradish Sauce

- 1½ tablespoons horseradish
- 1 teaspoon onion juice
- 2 teaspoons white vinegar
- ½ teaspoon sugar
- ½ teaspoon dry mustard
- 1 teaspoon salt
- 1 cup sour cream
- ½ cup mayonnaise

Drain beet juice into saucepan. Soften gelatin in juice and add vinegar, sugar, onion, salt, and Tabasco. Heat until gelatin is dissolved. Add beets and pour into 2½-cup oiled mold. Chill until set.

To prepare sauce, thoroughly blend horseradish, onion juice, vinegar, sugar, mustard, and salt. Add sour cream and mayonnaise and serve with mold.

♣

Beet Salad Ring

"Colorful."
Corinne L. Peterson

Serves: 8 to 10
Refrigerate: until set

- 2 16-ounce cans diced, cooked beets with juice
- 2 packages lemon-flavored gelatin
- ⅓ cup red wine vinegar
- 1 teaspoon grated onion
- 2½ teaspoons horseradish
- 1 cup diced celery

Bring beet juice and enough water to make 3 cups liquid to a boil and dissolve lemon gelatin. Add vinegar, onion, and horseradish. Chill until mixture thickens. Add beets and celery. Pour into 1½-quart, greased ring mold. Refrigerate until firm.

♣

Cold Broccoli Salad

"Best if prepared up to 8 hours ahead."
Sharon C. Davis

Serves: 8 to 10

- 3 pounds broccoli, cleaned and cut into spears
- ½ cup olive oil
- ¼ cup lemon juice
- ½ teaspoon salt
- Dash pepper
- 2 teaspoons chervil
- ½ cup salted cashews, coarsely broken

Cook broccoli until just tender, about 6 to 8 minutes. Place in serving dish. Combine olive oil, lemon juice, salt, pepper, and chervil. Pour over broccoli and chill. Just before serving, sprinkle with cashews.

♣

Green Bean, Walnut, and Feta Salad

"Fresh and crunchy."
Marilynn S. Tanguay

Serves: 6

- 1½ to 2 pounds green beans, halved crosswise
- ¾ cup olive oil
- ⅓ cup parsley, chopped
- ¼ cup white vinegar
- ¾ teaspoon salt
- ¼ teaspoon freshly ground pepper
- ½ teaspoon minced garlic
- 1 cup chopped, toasted walnuts
- 1 cup diced red onion
- 1 cup crumbled Feta cheese

Drop beans into 4 quarts boiling water and cook until tender but crisp, about 4 minutes. Drain well, rinse in cold water to stop cooking, and pat dry in paper towels. Combine oil, parsley, vinegar, salt, pepper, and garlic in blender or processor. (May be done ahead up to this point.) Arrange beans in serving dish and sprinkle with nuts, onion, and cheese. Just before serving, pour dressing over salad.

♣

Taboulah

"May be made a day or two ahead, but add tomatoes just before serving."
The Cookbook Committee

Serves: 4

- ¾ cup bulghur wheat
- ¾ cup finely chopped parsley
- 3 to 4 tablespoons finely chopped mint
- 3 medium tomatoes, finely chopped
- 1 medium onion, minced
- ¼ cup olive oil
- ¼ cup lemon juice
- 1 teaspoon salt
- Pinch pepper
- Pinch allspice
- Pinch crushed red pepper

Cover bulghur with water and soak for a few hours or overnight. Drain well. Stir in parsley, mint, tomatoes, and onion. Mix together olive oil, lemon juice, salt, pepper, allspice, and red pepper. Add to bulghur mixture and toss lightly. Serve chilled on lettuce or as sandwich on Syrian bread.

♣

Apricot Mold

"Attractive and delicious."
Mrs. Jarrel G. Burrow

Serves: 10 to 12
Refrigerate: until set

- 1 46-ounce can apricot nectar
- 4 3½-ounce packages apricot Jello
- 1 4-ounce jar junior baby food strained apricots
- 1 pint sour cream

Bring nectar to a boil, add Jello, and dissolve. Add strained apricots and mix well. Put half of mixture into large, glass bowl and refrigerate until set. Spread sour cream on top, and drizzle remaining Jello mixture over it. Refrigerate until ready to serve.

♣

Hawaiian Chicken Salad Supreme

"For curry lovers."
Janet Tranquada

Serves: 12
Refrigerate: several hours

- 2 quarts coarsely cut, cooked chicken or turkey
- 20 ounces water chestnuts, sliced
- 2 pounds seedless grapes
- 2 cups sliced celery
- 2 cups slivered, toasted almonds
- 3 cups mayonnaise
- 1 tablespoon curry powder
- 2 tablespoons soy sauce
- 2 tablespoons lemon juice (optional)
- Boston or bibb lettuce
- 1 large can (#2½) pineapple chunks, or 1 20-ounce can litchis

Mix together chicken, water chestnuts, grapes, celery, and 1 cup almonds. Mix mayonnaise with curry, soy, and lemon juice. Combine with chicken mixture and chill for several hours. Spoon into nests of lettuce. Sprinkle with remaining almonds and garnish with pineapple chunks.

♣

Chicken and Avocado Salad

"Tarragon is a great summer flavor."
Julie Martin Sanders

Serves: 4

- 1 ripe avocado, peeled and cubed
- Juice of 1 lemon
- 3 cups boned, cubed, cooked chicken
- 1 cup mayonnaise
- ½ cup minced parsley
- ½ to 1 teaspoon dried tarragon
- Salt and pepper to taste
- 6 bacon strips, cooked and crumbled

Toss avocado with lemon juice. Mix in remaining ingredients and serve immediately. Or, mix all but bacon and avocado, and refrigerate. Add bacon and avocado when ready to serve.

♣

Chinese Chicken Salad

"Different, light, tasty."
Mrs. Robert C. Slyder

Serves: 6
Bake: about 40 minutes at 325°F

Dressing

- 5 tablespoons rice vinegar, or 4 tablespoons cider vinegar
- 2 tablespoons sherry
- 1 teaspoon dry mustard
- 4 tablespoons sugar
- 1 tablespoon plus 1 teaspoon soy sauce
- ½ cup salad oil
- 1 tablespoon plus 1 teaspoon sesame oil

- 2 large chicken breasts, split
- Butter
- Paprika
- Oil
- 2 or 3 ounces rice sticks (maifun)
- 1 large head lettuce (thinly sliced)

To make dressing, combine first 5 ingredients and mix well. Add oils and mix again.

Dot chicken with butter and paprika. Bake with skin at 325°F for about 40 minutes, turning occasionally. Cool, remove skin, and cut chicken into thin strips. Marinate strips in some of dressing. In frying pan, heat 2 inches oil at medium high. Fry rice sticks a few at a time. As they puff, flip them and they will puff again. Drain on paper towels. Toss chicken, lettuce, rice sticks, and remaining dressing.

♣

Curried Chicken Salad with Fruit

"Superb luncheon dish."
Margaret C. Heald

Serves: 6
Refrigerate: 2 hours

- 3 cups cooked, chopped chicken
- 1 cup chopped celery
- 1 teaspoon salt
- 1 tablespoon lemon juice
- 1 cup seedless green grapes, halved
- 1 11-ounce can mandarin oranges, drained
- 1 cup mayonnaise
- 2 teaspoons curry powder
- 1 tablespoon soy sauce
- Salad greens
- Slivered toasted almonds

Mix chicken, celery, salt, and lemon juice with half of grapes and oranges. To make dressing, combine mayonnaise, curry powder, and soy sauce. Toss chicken mixture with dressing and refrigerate for at least 2 hours. Serve chicken on salad greens and garnish with remaining oranges and grapes. Top with toasted almonds.

♣

Curried Turkey Salad in Cantaloupe Halves

"The chutney makes it especially tasty."
Joan B. Dean

Serves: 6

- 1 cup mayonnaise
- 2 teaspoons curry
- 3½ pounds turkey breast, cooked and cubed
- 1½ cups thinly sliced celery
- ¾ cup mango chutney
- Salt and pepper to taste
- 3 cantaloupes

Condiments

- ½ pound toasted cashews
- ½ cup minced scallions
- ½ cup chopped red and green pepper
- ½ cup golden raisins
- ½ cup chopped dates

In large bowl, combine mayonnaise and curry thoroughly. Mix in turkey, celery, chutney, salt, and pepper. When ready to serve, spoon salad into cantaloupe halves. Serve each condiment in a separate bowl.

♣

Chicken and Rice Salad

"Delicious for a picnic."
Janet Tranquada

Serves: 10

- 1 6- to 7-ounce package chicken-flavored rice mix
- 2 green onions, including tops, thinly sliced
- ½ green pepper, seeded and chopped
- 8 pimento-stuffed olives, thinly sliced
- 2 6-ounce jars marinated artichoke hearts
- ½ cup mayonnaise
- ½ teaspoon curry powder
- 3 cups cooked, cubed chicken breasts

Cook rice as directed, omitting butter. Remove from heat, turn into bowl, and let cool to room temperature. Add onions, pepper, and olives. Drain artichoke hearts, reserving marinade. Combine marinade with mayonnaise and curry and blend thoroughly. Add to rice mixture. Add chicken and toss well. Thinly slice artichoke hearts and fold into mixture. Cover and refrigerate. Note: If "cara mia" hearts are used, use marinade from 1 jar and increase mayonnaise by 3 tablespoons.

♣

Sour Cream Strawberry Salad

"Nice for brunch or buffet."
Mrs. Robert C. Slyder

Serves: 8

- 1 pint fresh strawberries
- 1 cup sugar
- 1 tablespoon lemon juice
- 2 cups sour cream
- ½ cup confectioners' sugar

Wash, hull, and drain berries. Crush enough to make 1 cup. Sweeten with ⅓ cup sugar and add lemon juice. Stir remaining sugar into sour cream and mix well. Fold in crushed berries. Pour into small ring mold and freeze. Before serving, unmold onto platter. Pour confectioners' sugar over remaining berries and mix well. Pour into center of salad and serve immediately.

♣

Pineapple and Bean Salad

"A different and really pretty bean salad."
Adelaide S. Bennett

Serves: 10 to 14

- 1 14-ounce can pineapple chunks, drained, with liquid reserved
- 1 16-ounce can red kidney beans, drained and rinsed
- 1 10-ounce package frozen lima beans, cooked until barely tender
- 1 10-ounce package frozen green beans, cooked until barely tender
- 1 green pepper, chopped
- 1 cup sliced celery

Dressing

- ½ cup pineapple liquid
- 1 tablespoon cornstarch
- ¼ cup wine vinegar
- 1 tablespoon dry mustard
- ½ teaspoon pepper
- ½ teaspoon dill
- 2 teaspoons sugar
- 1 teaspoon seasoned salt
- ¼ cup olive oil

Place salad ingredients in bowl and chill.

To make dressing, blend all ingredients, except oil, in saucepan over medium heat until thickened. Remove from heat and beat in oil. When cool, add to salad and serve.

Lemons
Linda Plotkin (American b. 1938)
Soft-ground etching, roulette work, and drypoint, 25.6 x 24.6 cm
Gift of Mrs. Helen Sagoff Slosberg, 1980.6

♣

Lemon Mold with Orange Marmalade

"Nice tart, lemon flavor."
Riva T. Grace

Serves: 8
Refrigerate: until set

- 1 6-ounce package lemon Jello
- 2 cups boiling water
- 1 6-ounce can frozen lemonade
- 5 ounces Cool Whip
- ⅓ cup orange marmalade

Dissolve Jello in boiling water, add lemonade, and blend. Chill until slightly thickened. Beat in Cool Whip. Add marmalade and pour into 4-cup mold. Refrigerate. Unmold when ready to serve.

♣

Lemon-Rice Mold

"Good as salad or dessert."
Mrs. Edward J. Doherty, Jr.

Serves: 6
Refrigerate: until set

- 1 3½-ounce package lemon Jello
- 1 cup boiling water
- 1 cup drained, crushed pineapple, with juice reserved
- Dash salt
- 2 cups cooked rice, cooled
- 1 cup whipped cream
- 4 tablespoons sugar

Dissolve Jello in water. Add pineapple juice and salt. Refrigerate. When Jello starts to thicken slightly, whip until frothy. Add cooked rice, whipped cream sweetened with sugar, and crushed pineapple. Pour into 4-cup mold. Refrigerate until set. When ready to serve, unmold.

♣

Pineapple-Cherry Mold

"A real holiday treat."
Mrs. John F. Buckley

Serves: 10 to 12
Refrigerate: several hours

- 2 envelopes gelatin
- ¼ cup cold water
- 1 20-ounce can crushed pineapple
- Juice of 1 lemon
- 1 8-ounce package cream cheese, softened
- 1 cup sugar
- 1 6-ounce jar maraschino cherries, chopped and juice reserved
- ½ pint whipping cream

Soften gelatin in cold water. Heat pineapple with juices from can and add to gelatin. Add lemon juice. Chill to consistency of egg white. Beat cream cheese with sugar and cherry juice until very smooth. In separate bowl, beat cream until stiff. Fold cream cheese mixture, whipped cream, and cherries into pineapple mixture, until all ingredients are thoroughly blended. Pour into greased 8-cup mold and chill several hours. Just before serving, loosen edge with knife, dip quickly in warm water, and unmold.

Still Life, 1658
Joris van Son (Flemish 1623–1667)
Oil on canvas, 55.6 x 45.9 cm
1983.39

Breads

Sculptured Brioche

"Beautiful for a holiday brunch."
Judith Parker Vander Salm

Yield: 1 large ring or 2 braided loaves
Rising time: about 1½ hours
Bake: 30 minutes at 350°F

- 2 packages dry yeast
- ⅓ cup warm water
- ⅓ cup milk
- ¾ cup butter
- ½ cup sugar
- 1 teaspoon salt
- ½ teaspoon nutmeg
- Grated rind of ½ lemon
- 5 large eggs
- 5 cups flour

Glaze

- 1 egg yolk
- 1 tablespoon water

Blend yeast with warm water and let stand 5 minutes until dissolved. Heat milk and butter together until butter is melted and mixture is lukewarm. Pour into bowl and add yeast. Stir in sugar, salt, nutmeg, lemon, and eggs. Blend in 4 cups flour, or more if dough remains sticky. Cover bowl with damp cloth and let rise until double, about 1 hour.

For ring-shaped brioche, place small, greased bowl upside down on greased baking sheet. Divide dough into thirds and make 3 long coils by rolling dough back and forth on board using palms of your hands. Attach ends of coils together and braid around bowl, forming ring.

For 2 braided loaves, halve dough and make 3 coils from each half. Braid into oblong loaves and place on greased cookie sheet.

After braiding, let dough rise until puffy, about 30 minutes. Beat yolk with water and brush dough with glaze. Bake at 350°F for 30 minutes. Let cool on pan. Serve with jelly or Brie.

Processor Brioche

"Time consuming, but sure to be a success!"
Patricia Leonard Bagg

Yield: 16 to 20
Rising time: 2 hours and 30 minutes
Refrigerate: 4 hours or overnight
Bake: 12 to 15 minutes at 425°F and 10 minutes at 350°F

- 1 package yeast
- 1/4 cup water at 105° to 115°F
- 1 cup unsalted butter, room temperature
- 3 tablespoons sugar
- 1/2 teaspoon salt
- 4 large eggs, room temperature
- 3 3/4 cups flour
- Melted butter

Glaze

- 1 egg
- 1 tablespoon water

Proof yeast in water and let stand 5 minutes. Using steel blade, cream butter with sugar and salt for 1 minute. Scrape bowl and cream 1 more minute. Add yeast mixture and process 10 seconds. Add eggs, 1 at a time, pulsing on and off twice. Add 2 cups flour, 1 at a time, processing 10 seconds between each. Add third cup flour and process 1 minute. If machine starts to slow down, switch to plastic mixing blade. Add remaining flour and process 10 seconds. Rest dough 5 minutes, then process 15 seconds. Repeat. Scrape dough, which should be very soft and sticky, into well-buttered bowl.

Brush surface with melted butter. Cover with plastic wrap and let rise until double, about 1 1/2 hours. Stir dough down and beat hard until it forms a ball. Cover and let rise again until double, about 1 hour. Stir down and refrigerate at least 4 hours or overnight. Punch down again. To shape dough, butter molds and hands. Roll dough into golf-sized balls and put in molds. Make indentation in top, roll dough into marble-sized balls, and insert into top. Cover and let rise until double, 1 to 1 1/2 hours. Beat egg with water and brush top with glaze. Don't let glaze run down sides. Bake at 425°F for 12 to 15 minutes, until puffed and golden brown. Bake at 350°F for 10 more minutes. Remove from molds and cool on racks. Note: Baked brioche freezes well. If machine won't knead all the dough at once, knead 1/2 at a time.

Irish Soda Bread

"Delicious buttered and with a good cup of coffee."
Pat O'Brien

Yield: 2 loaves
Bake: 50 to 60 minutes at 350°F

- 4 cups flour
- 1 cup sugar
- 1 teaspoon salt
- 1 teaspoon baking soda
- 3/4 cup butter
- 1 1/3 cups buttermilk
- 1 cup raisins
- 1 tablespoon caraway seeds

Mix flour, sugar, salt, and baking soda together and cut butter into mixture. Add buttermilk, raisins, and caraway seeds. Knead for 1 minute on floured board. Halve dough and form 2 rounds. Place loaves on long cookie sheet and bake at 350°F for 50 to 60 minutes. Bread is done when knife is inserted and comes out clean.

Food Processor White Bread

"For people who can't get enough homemade bread."
Mrs. Dix F. Davis

Yield: 2 loaves
Rising time: 2 hours and 30 minutes
Bake: 10 minutes at 450°F and 30 minutes at 350°F

- 1 tablespoon dry yeast
- ½ cup lukewarm water
- 6 cups flour
- 2½ teaspoons salt
- 2 tablespoons sugar
- 1½ teaspoons shortening
- 1½ teaspoons butter
- 1 cup hot water
- 1 cup milk

Grease 1 large bowl and 2 loaf pans. Place yeast in water, stir, and let sit for 5 minutes. Place ½ each flour, salt, sugar, shortening, and butter in food processor with steel blade. Combine ½ hot water and ½ milk in measuring cup. With food processor on, add ½ yeast mixture and as much of milk mixture as is necessary to make large ball of dough, usually about ⅞ cup. Remove dough and place in large greased bowl. To make dough for second loaf, repeat above procedure with remaining ingredients. Cover bowl and let rise for 1 hour. Punch down dough and knead on floured surface for 2 minutes. Place dough back in greased bowl and let rise, covered with cloth, for 45 minutes. Punch down, halve, knead for 1 minute, and shape into loaves. Place each loaf in greased bread pan, and let rise, covered with damp towel, for 45 more minutes. Bake at 450°F for 10 minutes. Reduce heat to 350°F and bake 30 more minutes. Remove bread from pans immediately and, for soft crust, brush top with melted butter. Note: This recipe is so simple to make, it can easily be doubled for 4 loaves.

Whole Grain Banana Bread

"A healthy, hearty bread."
Jessica Reynolds Jenner

Yield: 1 loaf
Bake: 45 to 60 minutes at 350°F

- ⅓ cup honey
- 6 tablespoons margarine
- 2 eggs
- 2 overripe bananas
- 1½ cups unsifted, whole wheat pastry flour
- ¼ cup wheat germ
- ¼ cup soy granules, or finely chopped nuts
- 1 teaspoon baking soda

Beat honey and margarine together until creamy. Add eggs, 1 at a time, beating after each. Mash bananas with fork and add 1 at a time. In separate bowl, stir together remaining ingredients. Add to banana mixture and stir gently. Pour batter into well-greased loaf pan and bake at 350°F for 45 to 60 minutes, or until top springs back when lightly touched.

Oatmeal-Nut Bread

"Excellent for toasting."
Mrs. David J. Milliken

Yield: 3 loaves
Rising time: about 2 hours
Bake: 30 minutes at 400°F

- 9 cups unsifted flour
- 2 teaspoons salt
- 2 packages Fleischmann's dry yeast
- 1 cup water
- ½ cup milk
- ½ cup molasses
- ½ cup margarine
- 2 eggs (room temperature)
- 2 cups cooked old-fashioned oatmeal
- 1 cup chopped pecans

In bowl, combine 2 cups flour, salt, and yeast. Over low heat, bring water, milk, molasses, and margarine to 120° to 130°F. Add to dry ingredients and beat 2 minutes at medium speed, scraping sides of bowl occasionally. Add eggs, oatmeal, and 1 cup flour. Beat at high speed 2 minutes. Stir in enough flour to make dough stiff. Turn onto floured board and knead 8 to 10 minutes. Place in warm, greased bowl. Grease top of dough and cover, first with waxed paper or plastic wrap and then with clean, damp tea towel. Let rise until double, about 1 hour. Punch down and knead in pecans. Divide dough into 3 equal parts. Shape into loaves and place in 3 greased loaf pans. Cover with damp towel and let rise until double, about 1 hour. Bake at 400°F for 30 minutes or until wire tester comes out clean.

Cranberry-Orange Bread

"A natural for Thanksgiving dinner."
Elizabeth C. Sullivan

Yield: 1 loaf
Bake: 1 hour at 325°F

- Juice and grated rind of 1 orange
- 2 tablespoons butter
- Boiling water
- 2 cups flour
- ½ teaspoon salt
- ½ teaspoon baking soda
- 1½ teaspoons baking powder
- 1 cup sugar
- 1 egg, well beaten
- ½ cup chopped nuts
- 1 cup raw cranberries

Mix together orange juice, rind, and butter in measuring cup. Add enough boiling water to make ¾ cup liquid and let stand until ready to use. In large bowl, mix together flour, salt, baking soda, baking powder, and sugar. Stir in egg and orange mixture until blended. Lightly flour nuts and cranberries and fold into batter. Pour into greased loaf pan and bake at 325°F for 1 hour.

La Glaneuse, 1885
Lucien Dautrey (French 1851–1926)
after Jules Breton (French 1827–1905)
Etching, 62.2 x 34.3 cm
Gift of Mrs. Kingsmill Marrs,
1925.1053

Strawberry Bread

"A springtime treat."
Helen Spool

Yield: 2 loaves
Bake: 1 hour at 350°F

- 2 cups fresh, sliced strawberries, or 1 16-ounce package frozen, unsweetened strawberries
- 2 cups sugar
- 4 eggs
- 1¼ cups vegetable oil
- 3 cups flour
- 1 teaspoon baking soda
- 1 teaspoon salt
- 2 teaspoons cinnamon
- 1 cup chopped nuts

Sprinkle strawberries with ½ cup sugar and let stand until juices form. Add eggs and oil and stir. In separate bowl, mix together flour, baking soda, salt, cinnamon, remaining sugar, and nuts. Add dry ingredients to strawberry mixture and stir until just blended. Pour into 2 greased loaf pans and bake at 350°F for 1 hour. Serve with cream cheese or butter.

Mango Bread

"Wonderful tropical flavor."
Sarah Cederbaum Ribeiro

Yield: 2 loaves
Bake: 40 to 60 minutes at 350°F

- 2 cups flour
- 1½ cups sugar
- 2 teaspoons cinnamon
- 2 teaspoons baking soda
- ½ teaspoon salt
- 1 teaspoon vanilla
- 3 eggs
- ½ cup vegetable oil
- ½ cup margarine
- ½ cup raisins
- ½ cup coconut
- 2 cups chopped, ripe mangos

Mix all ingredients in bowl and pour into 2 greased loaf pans. Let stand for 20 minutes. Bake at 350°F for 40 to 60 minutes. Bread is done when wire tester comes out clean.

Woman with a Pear
Ferdinand Bol (Dutch 1616–1680)
Etching, 14.5 x 12 cm
Edward A. Bigelow Collection,
gift of Mrs. Robert M. Heberton,
1981.218

Pumpkin Bread

"The best pumpkin bread you'll ever eat."
Jill O. Howe

Yield: 2 loaves
Bake: 1 hour and 30 minutes at 350°F

- 4 cups flour
- 3 cups sugar
- 2 teaspoons baking soda
- 1 teaspoon baking powder
- 1 teaspoon cinnamon
- 1 teaspoon nutmeg
- 1 teaspoon allspice
- 1 teaspoon ginger
- 1 cup pure vegetable oil
- ⅔ cup cold water
- 1 15-ounce can pumpkin
- 4 eggs

In large bowl, mix dry ingredients. Blend in oil, water, pumpkin, and eggs. Pour into 2 greased loaf pans and bake at 350°F for 1 hour and 30 minutes. Note: This bread freezes well and keeps a long time.

Indian Corn Bread

"Delightfully different."
Zabelle D'Amico

Yield: 1 loaf
Bake: 1 hour at 350°F

- 1½ cups unsifted all-purpose flour
- 3 teaspoons baking powder
- 1 teaspoon salt
- ½ cup sugar
- ¼ cup butter, softened
- 2 eggs
- 1 cup canned pumpkin
- ½ cup milk
- 1 cup yellow corn meal
- 1 cup frozen blueberries, thawed and drained
- ½ cup chopped walnuts

Preheat oven to 350°F and lightly grease 9 x 5-inch loaf pan. Sift together flour, baking powder, and salt and set aside. In large bowl using rotary beater, beat sugar, butter, and eggs until smooth. Add pumpkin, milk, and corn meal and beat again. Add flour mixture and stir until just combined. Gently stir in blueberries and nuts. Pour into greased, floured pan and bake at 350°F for 1 hour or until toothpick inserted in center comes out clean. Let cool in pan or on rack for 10 minutes before cutting.

Orange Marmalade Bread

"Good English marmalade makes this especially piquant."
Elizabeth Trumbull Bright

Yield: 1 loaf
Bake: 1 hour at 350°F

- 2½ cups flour
- 1 teaspoon salt
- 1 teaspoon baking soda
- ¾ cup sugar
- 1 egg
- ½ cup marmalade
- ¼ cup vinegar
- 1 cup milk
- 2 tablespoons melted shortening

Sift together flour, salt, baking soda, and sugar and set aside. In separate bowl, combine egg and marmalade. Add vinegar, milk, and shortening. Combine both mixtures quickly and lightly. Pour into greased loaf pan and bake at 350°F for 1 hour.

Cinnamon-Raisin Bread

"An old family recipe."
Mrs. Israel S. Morin

Yield: 3 loaves
Rising time: about 3 hours
Bake: 45 minutes at 375°F

- 3 packages dry yeast
- ¾ cup warm water
- 1 cup plus 2 teaspoons sugar
- 8 cups plus 2 tablespoons flour
- 1 cup butter
- 3 eggs
- 1¼ cups milk
- 1 tablespoon salt
- Sugar, cinnamon, and raisins

In small bowl, mix yeast, water, 2 teaspoons sugar, and 2 tablespoons flour. Cover and set aside to proof. Put remaining flour in large bowl and cut in butter. Add eggs, milk, salt, and remaining sugar and mix thoroughly. Add yeast mixture and mix again. Put dough in well-greased bowl and turn to coat. Cover and let rise until double in bulk, about 2 hours. Punch down and place on lightly floured board. Let rest for 5 minutes. Roll out with rolling pin until dough measures about 15 x 20 inches. If dough is too sticky to work with, add a little extra flour. Mix sugar, cinnamon, and raisins, adjusting sweetness to taste, and sprinkle on dough.

Roll up dough jelly-roll style and cut into thirds. Place each piece in greased 8-inch loaf pan. Cover and let rise again until double in bulk, about 1 hour. Bake at 375°F for 45 minutes. Remove from oven and let cool in pans for a few minutes. Remove from pans and finish cooling on wire rack.

Fruit-Bran Muffins

"Nutritious and delicious for breakfast."
Mrs. Kalman S. Sinofsky

Yield: 12 to 16 muffins
Bake: 25 to 30 minutes at 400°F

- 1¼ cups all-bran cereal
- ¼ cup unprocessed bran
- 1¼ cups milk
- ⅓ cup butter, softened
- ¼ cup sugar
- ¼ cup brown sugar
- 1 egg, lightly beaten
- 3 tablespoons dark molasses
- 1¼ cups flour
- 3 teaspoons baking powder
- ½ teaspoon salt
- 1½ teaspoons cinnamon
- 1 teaspoon allspice
- ¼ teaspoon ground cloves
- ¼ teaspoon nutmeg
- ¼ cup chopped dates
- ¼ cup raisins
- 6 to 8 maraschino cherries, halved

In bowl, soften brans with milk for 10 minutes. Cream butter and sugars. Beat in egg. Stir in bran mixture and molasses. Add dry ingredients and mix well. Stir in dates and raisins. Grease muffin tins or line with paper baking cups. Fill cups ⅔ full and top with cherry. Bake at 400°F for 25 to 30 minutes. Note: Unprocessed bran can be found at health food stores.

Scottish Oatcakes

"An unusual accompaniment to a 'country' meal."
Nancy N. Nesbitt

Yield: 20 squares
Bake: 12 to 15 minutes at 375°F

- 1 cup flour
- 1 tablespoon sugar
- ½ teaspoon salt
- 1 teaspoon baking powder
- 2 cups rolled oats
- ½ cup softened butter
- ½ cup milk

Preheat oven to 375°F. Sift together flour, sugar, salt, and baking powder. Stir in rolled oats. Cut in softened butter until well blended. Gradually add milk, mixing thoroughly. Roll out on greased cookie sheet until dough is about ⅛-inch thick. Bake at 375°F for 12 to 15 minutes, until golden brown. Cut into squares and serve plain or with butter. Note: These should be crispy.

Woman Preparing a Meal, 1768
Jacob Cornelis Ploos van Amstel
(Dutch 1726–1798) after Gabriel
Metsu (Dutch 1629–1667)
Crayon manner print, 29.5 x 21.1 cm
Bequest of Mrs. Kingsmill Marrs,
1926.1450

Carrot Muffins

"Perfect for a fall dinner."
Mrs. Elias S. Grace

Yield: 6 large muffins
Bake: 30 to 45 minutes at 350°F

- ¾ cup vegetable shortening
- ½ cup brown sugar
- 1 egg
- 1 tablespoon water
- 1¼ cups flour
- 1 teaspoon baking powder
- ½ teaspoon baking soda
- ½ teaspoon nutmeg
- ½ teaspoon cinnamon
- ½ teaspoon salt
- 2 cups grated carrots

Cream shortening and brown sugar. Beat egg with water and add to sugar mixture. Combine dry ingredients and add to mixture. Add grated carrots and stir until thoroughly blended. Pour into 6 greased ovenproof custard cups and bake at 350°F for 30 to 45 minutes until golden brown. Note: This can be served as a vegetable.

Squash Rolls

"Delightful for a fall menu."
Mrs. John F. Buckley

Yield: 24
Rising time: 2 hours
Bake: 15 to 20 minutes at 375°F

- 1 package dry yeast
- ¼ cup warm water
- Pinch sugar
- 1 cup scalded milk
- 1 cup boiling water
- ½ cup firmly packed brown sugar
- ¼ cup butter, softened and cut in pieces
- 1½ teaspoons salt
- 1 cup winter squash, cooked and strained
- 2 egg yolks, lightly beaten
- 1 egg, lightly beaten
- 1 teaspoon grated lemon rind
- 6 cups flour

In small bowl, proof yeast in warm water with sugar for 10 minutes. In large bowl, combine milk, boiling water, brown sugar, butter, and salt. Stir mixture until butter is melted. Let cool until lukewarm. Add squash, yeast mixture, yolks, egg, and lemon rind and mix well. Beat in flour ½ cup at a time until dough is soft and sticky and leaves side of bowl. Cover dough and let rise in warm place until double in bulk, about 1 hour and 30 minutes. Punch down. With buttered fingers, pinch off egg-sized pieces of dough and place in 24 buttered muffin cups. Cover and let rise until double, about 30 minutes. Bake rolls in preheated oven at 375°F for 15 to 20 minutes, until browned.

Cheoreg

"This traditional Armenian biscuit is good with any meal, and in between."
Mrs. N. John Kabian

Yield: 8 dozen
Rising time: about 6 hours
Bake: 15 to 20 minutes at 350°F

- 3 packages dry yeast
- Warm water
- 1 cup butter
- 1 cup vegetable shortening
- 2 cups milk
- 2 cups water
- 7 eggs
- 2 cups sugar
- 1 tablespoon salt
- 5 pounds all-purpose flour
- 1 to 2 eggs, beaten
- ¼ cup sesame seeds

Place yeast in enough warm water to dissolve. In saucepan, melt butter and shortening. In separate saucepan, combine milk and water and heat until warm. Beat 7 eggs in 10- or 15-quart bowl. Add sugar, salt, shortenings, and milk mixture, stirring thoroughly. Add yeast and blend. Gradually mix in flour. Knead dough until no longer sticky. Add more flour, if necessary, to achieve soft texture. Cover top and sides well with cloth and set in warm place to rise for 4 to 5 hours.

Turn dough onto lightly floured surface and keep covered with cloth to prevent from drying while forming biscuits. Take small ball of dough and roll it between palms to form 8-inch strip, about ½ inch thick. Start with 3-inch circle and coil dough upward 2½ times, making each turn slightly smaller. There should be a "tail" of dough left over. Run it down outside of biscuit and tuck end under. Ideally, end of dough should fill in open space at top of spiral. A second way to form biscuits is to fold 8-inch strip in half, joining ends, and twisting into oblong braid.

Place on Teflon or greased cookie sheet, allowing enough room between cheoreg for further rising. Brush tops with egg and sprinkle lightly with sesame seeds. Let stand 2 hours in warm place. Bake at 350°F for 15 to 20 minutes, until light golden brown.

Note: This is a very versatile bread and can be made into any shape desired. Raisins, candied fruit, or cinnamon and sugar can be added for a sweeter flavor.

Cream Muffins

"Rich and delicious."
Lilyan Bachrach

Yield: 12 muffins
Bake: 12 minutes at 425°F

- 2 eggs, separated
- 1 cup heavy cream
- 1 cup sifted flour
- Butter

Stir egg yolks with fork and mix in cream. Add flour and beat until perfectly smooth. Beat egg whites and gently fold into batter. Butter muffin tin liberally and fill cups ½ to ⅔ full. Bake at 425°F for 12 minutes. Serve immediately and toast any leftovers next day.

Quickie-Sticky Pecan Rolls

"A quick version of a traditional favorite."
Karson Aubuchon

Yield: 32 small rolls
Bake: 20 to 25 minutes at 375°F

- 8 tablespoons butter, softened
- ¾ cup brown sugar
- ¼ cup water
- ½ cup chopped pecans
- 2 8-ounce cans crescent dinner rolls
- 2 teaspoons cinnamon
- ¼ cup sugar

Preheat oven to 375°F. In 13 x 9-inch pan, melt 5 tablespoons butter in oven. Stir brown sugar, water, and pecans into butter. Separate each can of crescent dough into 4 rectangles and seal perforations in dough. Spread each rectangle with remaining butter. Combine cinnamon and sugar and sprinkle over buttered dough. Starting at shorter edge, roll up each rectangle. Cut each roll into 4 slices, forming 32 pieces in all. Arrange cut side down on pecan mixture. Bake at 375°F for 20 to 25 minutes or until golden brown. Invert pan to remove rolls. Serve warm. Note: If 32 rolls are too many for your family, halve recipe and use an 8-inch, round cake pan.

Welsh Griddle Cakes

"Interesting and unusual for tea."
Mrs. David J. Milliken

- 3 cups sifted flour
- 1 cup sugar
- 1½ teaspoons baking powder
- 1¼ teaspoons salt
- ½ teaspoon baking soda
- 2 teaspoons nutmeg
- 1 cup shortening
- 1 cup currants
- 2 eggs
- 6 tablespoons milk

Sift dry ingredients into bowl. Cut in shortening with pastry blender or food processor. Add currants. Beat eggs and milk until just blended. Add to dough and blend thoroughly. Cover and chill at least 1 hour. On floured board, roll out to ¼ inch thick and cut with cookie cutter. Heat griddle or frying pan slowly to medium and grease lightly. Bake cakes slowly until tops puff and turn shiny. Turn and bake other side. Serve hot or cold for tea or as breakfast roll.

Untitled, from the series *Urban Landscapes*, 1972
Richard Estes (American b. 1936)
Color silkscreen, 34.3 x 51.4 cm
Museum purchase, 1977.90

Desserts

*

Royal Marble Cheesecake

"The crust makes this unique."
Wendy I. Kelly

Serves: 12
Bake: 10 minutes at 400°F and 1 hour at 300°F
Refrigerate: at least 8 hours

Crust

- ¾ cup flour
- 2 tablespoons sugar
- ¼ teaspoon salt
- ¼ cup butter
- 1 cup semisweet chocolate pieces, melted

Filling

- 3 8-ounce packages cream cheese
- 1 cup sugar
- ¼ cup flour
- 2 teaspoons vanilla
- 6 eggs
- 1 cup sour cream

To make crust, combine flour, sugar, and salt in mixing bowl. Cut in butter until very fine. Stir in 2 tablespoons melted chocolate, reserving remainder for filling. Press into bottom of 9- or 10-inch spring-form pan. Bake at 400°F for 10 minutes.

While crust is baking, beat cream cheese with sugar in processor or mixer until creamy. Blend in flour and vanilla. Add eggs, 1 at a time, beating well after each. Blend in sour cream. Blend 1¾ cups filling with reserved melted chocolate. Pour remaining filling over crust and top with spoonfuls of chocolate mixture. Cut through batter to marble. Place in 400°F oven and immediately reduce heat to 300°F. Bake 1 hour, turn oven off, and leave in oven 1 hour. Cool away from draft and refrigerate at least 8 hours. Unmold carefully upside down on platter.

*

Ricotta Cheesecake

"Perfect buffet dessert."
Sally R. Trottier

Yield: 50 pieces
Bake: 1 hour at 350°F

- 1 18½-ounce package yellow cake mix
- 2 pounds Ricotta cheese
- 4 eggs
- ¾ cup sugar
- 1 teaspoon lemon extract
- Chopped walnuts and cherries

Prepare batter according to package directions. Pour into 13 x 9 x 2-inch, greased, floured pan. Combine cheese, eggs, sugar, and lemon extract. Pour over cake batter. Bake at 350°F for about 1 hour. Remove from oven and sprinkle with chopped nuts. Press gently. Slice cake into small squares when completely cooled. Add cherry pieces for decoration and place in small, individual paper cups. Keep refrigerated and serve cold.

*

Honey-Almond Cake

"Very good small cake."
Frances Dewey

Serves: 6 to 8
Bake: about 25 minutes at 350°F

- 1 cup sifted all-purpose flour
- ½ teaspoon baking powder
- ½ teaspoon baking soda
- ¼ teaspoon salt
- 1 egg
- ½ cup plain yogurt
- ½ cup honey
- ⅓ cup butter, melted and cooled
- ½ teaspoon vanilla
- ⅔ cup sliced almonds

Honey–Almond Syrup

- ⅓ cup honey
- ⅓ cup light corn syrup
- ½ teaspoon almond extract

Sift together flour, baking powder, soda, and salt. Set aside. In large mixing bowl, beat egg, yogurt, honey, butter, and vanilla until smooth. Add flour mixture all at once and continue beating until smooth. Pour into buttered, 9-inch, spring-form pan. Bake at 350°F about 25 minutes, or until cake shrinks from edge of pan. Meanwhile, heat honey and corn syrup in saucepan until mixture reaches 225°F on candy thermometer. Remove from heat and stir in almond extract. While cake is hot, cover top with sliced almonds. Slowly pour syrup evenly over cake and let soak in. Broil 6 inches from heat until almonds are lightly toasted. Watch *very* carefully with oven door open. Cool completely on wire rack before releasing spring form.

Soused Apple Hill Cake

"A winner every time."
Mrs. A. Abbott Coblentz

Serves: 10
Bake: 1 hour at 325°F

- 4 cups peeled, cored, chopped baking apples
- 6 tablespoons Calvados, or Apple Jack (more if needed)
- 2 cups sugar
- ½ cup salad oil
- 2 eggs
- 2 cups flour
- 2 teaspoons cinnamon
- 2 teaspoons baking soda
- 1 teaspoon nutmeg
- 1 teaspoon salt
- ¼ teaspoon ground cloves
- 1 cup chopped walnuts
- 1 cup white raisins, plumped in hot water

As apples are chopped, put in bowl and add as much Calvados as they will absorb. With electric mixer, beat together sugar, oil, and eggs. In separate bowl, sift together flour, cinnamon, baking soda, nutmeg, salt, and cloves. Mix in walnuts and raisins. Combine apples with flour mixture. Pour batter over floured apples and mix well (mixture will be lumpy). Pour into oiled 9 x 13-inch baking pan. Bake at 325°F for 1 hour, until tests done. Serve warm or cold with whipped cream. Note: Be sure to combine ingredients in order given.

Grandma's Applesauce Cake

"Can be easily doubled."
Vera D. Gladding

Serves: 6
Bake: 45 to 55 minutes at 325°F

- 1 cup sugar
- ½ cup shortening
- 1 teaspoon baking soda
- 1 cup applesauce
- 1 cup sifted flour
- 1 teaspoon cinnamon
- ¼ teaspoon nutmeg
- ½ teaspoon ground cloves
- ½ teaspoon salt
- 1 cup raisins

Cream together sugar and shortening. Dissolve baking soda in applesauce and add to shortening. Sift together flour, spices, and salt. Add raisins to flour and combine with applesauce mixture. Pour into heavily greased and floured 8 x 8-inch baking pan. Bake at 325°F for 45 to 55 minutes.

Pistachio Cake

"Unique, rich, and moist."
Frances Crowley

Serves: 12 to 14
Bake: 45 minutes to 1 hour at 375°F

- 4 eggs
- 1 18½-ounce package yellow cake mix
- ½ cup oil
- ½ cup water
- ½ cup orange juice
- ¾ cup chocolate syrup

Frosting

- 1 pint heavy cream
- ½ of 3½-ounce package pistachio pudding mix

Blend in with cake mix, oil, water and juice.

Beat eggs. Blend in cake mix, oil, water, and juice. Pour ½ batter into greased, floured tube pan. Mix chocolate syrup into remaining batter, pour into pan, and swirl with knife. Bake at 375°F for 45 minutes to 1 hour. Cool before frosting.

To make frosting, whip cream with pudding mix until firm.

*

Cold Oven Pound Cake

"A real Southern treat."
Janice N. Poe

Serves: 10 to 12
Bake: 1 hour at 350°F

- 1 cup vegetable shortening
- 2 tablespoons butter
- 2 cups sugar
- 1 teaspoon vanilla
- 1 teaspoon lemon extract
- 6 eggs
- 2 cups sifted flour

Cream vegetable shortening and butter. Mix in sugar, blending until light and creamy. Add vanilla and lemon extract. Beat in eggs 1 at a time. Add flour, 1 cup at a time, mixing thoroughly. Spoon into greased, floured tube pan. Place in cold oven. Set temperature at 350°F and bake 1 hour.

*

Apricot Upside-Down Cake

"Iron skillet necessary."
Mrs. Dix F. Davis

Bake: 30 to 40 minutes at 350°F

- ¼ cup butter
- 1 cup light brown sugar
- 1 17-ounce can apricot halves, reserve 5 tablespoons syrup
- 3 eggs, separated
- 1 cup sugar
- 1 cup flour
- 1 teaspoon baking powder
- ½ teaspoon salt

Melt butter in heavy 10-inch iron skillet. Remove from heat and spread evenly with brown sugar. Arrange apricots hollow side up in skillet. In mixing bowl, beat egg yolks with fork. Add granulated sugar and apricot syrup. Sift flour, baking powder, and salt into egg yolk mixture. Beat egg whites and fold into batter. Pour over apricot halves in skillet. Bake at 350°F for 30 to 40 minutes. Set skillet on cooling rack for only 5 to 10 minutes before turning upside down on serving plate. Serve warm, topped with vanilla ice cream.

*

Lemon Yogurt Pound Cake

"Nutritious and always gets rave reviews."
Jean Connor

Serves: 12
Bake: about 1 hour at 325°F

- 2¼ cups flour
- 2 cups sugar
- ½ teaspoon salt
- ½ teaspoon baking soda
- 1 teaspoon grated lemon rind
- 1 teaspoon vanilla
- 1 cup softened butter
- 1 8-ounce container lemon yogurt
- 3 eggs

Glaze

- 1 cup confectioners' sugar
- 2 teaspoons lemon juice

In large mixing bowl, combine all cake ingredients with low speed of electric mixer. Increase to medium speed and beat 3 minutes, scraping bowl. Pour into greased, floured, 10-inch tube or bundt pan. Bake at 325°F for about 1 hour. Cool 15 minutes before removing from pan. Beat confectioners' sugar and lemon juice until smooth. Drizzle glaze over cooled cake.

*

Feather Cake

"Serve with ice cream or fresh fruit."
Mrs. Jacques J. Burguet

Serves: 6
Bake: 50 minutes at 350°F

- 1 cup sugar
- 3 eggs
- Pinch salt
- ½ teaspoon vanilla
- 1½ cups sifted, self-rising flour
- 1 cup cream, whipped

Lemon Icing

- 2 cups confectioners' sugar
- ¼ cup butter, softened
- Grated rind and juice of 1 lemon
- 1 to 2 teaspoons cream

Blend sugar and eggs well. Add salt and vanilla. Blend in flour. Slowly fold in whipped cream. Put in greased, floured, 8-inch pan and bake in 350°F preheated oven for 50 minutes. *Never* open oven door during baking. Cool on cake rack.

To make icing, blend sugar and butter. Beat in rind, juice, and cream. Spread on cake before cool.

*

Mississippi Mud

"For chocolate lovers."
Mrs. William Richardson

Serves: 10 to 12
Bake: 1 hour and 30 minutes at 275°F

- 2 cups flour
- 1 teaspoon soda
- Pinch salt
- 1¾ cups strong coffee
- ½ cup bourbon
- 5 ounces bitter chocolate, cut up
- 1 cup butter
- 2 cups sugar
- 2 eggs, lightly beaten
- 1 teaspoon vanilla

Sift together flour, soda, and salt. Heat coffee and bourbon in top of double boiler for 5 minutes. Add chocolate and butter, stirring until melted and smooth. Remove from heat, stir in sugar, and cool for 3 minutes. Transfer to bowl. Add flour mixture to chocolate ½ cup at a time. Continue to beat for 1 minute. Add eggs and vanilla, beating until smooth. Butter 9 x 3½-inch tube pan and dust with cocoa. Bake at 275°F for 1 hour and 30 minutes, or until tests done. Cool completely in pan. Serve with soft whipped cream. Note: Must be cool before cutting.

*

Georgia Peach Pie

"Use fresh, juicy peaches."
Mrs. John F. Reynders

Serves: 6
Bake: 1 hour at 350°F

- ½ cup butter
- 1 cup sugar
- 1 cup flour
- 1 teaspoon baking powder
- Juice of 1 lemon
- ⅔ cup milk
- 3 cups skinned, sliced peaches

Melt butter in 9 x 12 x 4-inch baking pan. Combine sugar, flour, baking powder, lemon juice, and milk thoroughly. Pour mixture into buttered pan and swirl. Arrange peaches on top. Bake at 350°F for 1 hour until brown. Serve warm with whipped or ice cream.

*

Appelpaj (Swedish Apple Pie)

"Good for a quick dessert and easy for those who can't make a good crust."
Virginia I. Harding

Serves: 8
Bake: 35 to 40 minutes at 350°F

- 4 cups sliced, cooking apples
- 1 tablespoon sugar
- 1 teaspoon cinnamon
- ½ cup chopped pecans, or walnuts
- ½ cup butter
- 1 cup sugar
- 1 egg, well beaten
- 1 cup sifted, all-purpose flour
- ¼ teaspoon salt
- 1 teaspoon double-acting baking powder
- Whipped cream

In buttered, 9-inch pie plate, spread sliced apples and sprinkle with sugar, cinnamon, and pecans. Cream butter and sugar until light. Beat in egg. Sift together flour, salt, and baking powder and add to creamed mixture. Spoon batter over apples and gently spread. Bake at 350°F for 35 to 40 minutes. Let cool in pan about 5 minutes. Turn pie upside down onto serving plate. Serve warm with whipped cream. Note: Can be "Americanized" by using vanilla ice cream.

*

Eggnog Pie

"Smooth and rich—a perfect holiday dessert."
Mary E. Manahan

Serves: 6 to 8
Refrigerate: 2 to 3 hours

- 2 cups eggnog
- 1 envelope unflavored gelatin
- 3 tablespoons cold water
- 1 cup heavy cream
- ¼ teaspoon salt
- ¼ cup sugar
- 2 teaspoons vanilla
- 1 graham cracker pie crust
- Dash nutmeg

Warm eggnog over medium heat. Dissolve gelatin in cold water and blend in eggnog until smooth. Chill until partially firm, 30 to 45 minutes, and whip lightly. In separate bowl, whip cream with salt, sugar, and vanilla. Gently fold in eggnog mixture. Pour into pie crust, sprinkle with nutmeg, and refrigerate a few hours.

*

Impossible Coconut Custard Pie

"Amazingly, the pie makes its own crust."
The Cookbook Committee

Serves: 6 to 8
Bake: 40 minutes at 350°F

- 4 eggs
- 2 cups milk
- ¾ cup sugar
- ½ cup flour
- Dash salt
- 1 teaspoon vanilla
- ¼ cup butter
- 1 cup coconut

Place ingredients in blender in order listed. Blend at high speed while counting to 10 slowly. Pour into greased, 9-inch pie plate. Bake at 350°F for 40 minutes.

*

Pie Crust

"Very flaky."
Deborah A. Atchue

Yield: 10-inch double crust

- 2½ cups flour
- 1 tablespoon sugar
- 1 teaspoon salt
- ½ pound lard
- 1 egg, beaten
- ½ cup milk

Sift together dry ingredients. Cut in lard until dough has coarse, crumb consistency. Mix in egg and milk. If dough is too sticky, add a little more flour. Note: Can be used with savory pies if sugar is omitted.

*

Chocolate-Pecan Pie

"Top with vanilla ice cream."
Sue Mills

Serves: 6 to 8
Bake: 50 minutes at 350°F

- 1 cup sugar
- 4 eggs
- 1 cup light corn syrup
- 1 teaspoon vanilla
- ½ cup butter, melted
- 1 6-ounce package chocolate chips
- 1 cup chopped pecans
- 1 10-inch, unbaked pie shell

Blend sugar, eggs, corn syrup, and vanilla thoroughly. Add butter, chips, and nuts. Pour into pie shell. Bake at 350°F for 50 minutes, or until set.

*

German Tart

"For anyone with a sweet tooth."
Edmond de Beaumont

Serves: 6
Bake: 1 hour at 350°F

- ½ cup butter
- ½ cup sugar
- 1 small egg
- ½ teaspoon vanilla
- ¼ teaspoon salt
- 1½ cups flour
- Fruit, sweetened to taste

Mix together butter, sugar, egg, vanilla, and salt. Work in as much flour as butter mixture needs to hold together. Handling dough as little as possible and using greased 9 x 9-inch pan, pat dough from thickness of ⅜ inch on bottom of pan to 1 inch high on sides of pan. Cover dough with fruit. Bake at 350°F for 1 hour, or until tart is nicely browned.

Créme de Menthe Pie

"Very rich."
The Cookbook Committee

Serves: 8
Bake crust: 7 minutes at 350°F
Freeze

- 25 chocolate wafers, crushed
- 1 tablespoon sugar
- ⅓ cup butter, melted
- 24 marshmallows
- ⅔ cup milk
- ¼ cup green créme de menthe
- 1 cup heavy cream, whipped
- Shaved semi-sweet chocolate, or crushed nuts and whipped cream (optional)

To make chocolate crumb crust, combine crushed cookies, sugar, and butter. Press mixture into greased, 9-inch pie plate covering bottom and sides. Bake crust at 350°F for 7 minutes. Cool. To make filling, combine marshmallows and milk in saucepan. Stir over low heat until marshmallows are melted. Cool. Fold in créme de menthe and whipped cream. Pour into cooled crust and freeze. Remove from freezer 20 minutes before serving. Garnish with chocolate.

Pumpkin Chiffon Pie

"A light and delicious change from pumpkin pie."
Robin D. Whitney

Serves: 8
Refrigerate

- 3 eggs, separated
- 1 cup sugar
- 1¼ cups cooked mashed pumpkin (canned is fine)
- ½ cup milk
- ½ teaspoon salt
- ½ teaspoon ground ginger
- ½ teaspoon nutmeg
- ½ teaspoon cinnamon
- 1 envelope unflavored gelatin
- ¼ cup water
- 1 10-inch graham cracker crust

Beat egg yolks with ½ sugar. Add pumpkin, milk, and spices. Cook in double boiler over simmering water until thick. Dissolve gelatin in water, add to pumpkin mixture, and refrigerate. Beat egg whites until stiff, adding remaining sugar gradually. When pumpkin mixture starts to get firm, fold in egg whites and pour into graham cracker crust. Refrigerate. When ready to serve, top with whipped cream and slivers of candied ginger.

Orange-Rhubarb Pie

"Wonderfully tart! The first sign of spring."
Ellen R. Berezin

Serves: 8
Bake: 10 minutes at 450°F and 40 to 50 minutes at 350°F

- Dough for 1 double crust pie
- 4 cups chopped fresh rhubarb
- 1½ cups sugar
- ½ cup orange juice
- 3 tablespoons flour
- 2 eggs
- 1½ teaspoons dried grated orange peel
- Pinch salt
- 1 to 2 tablespoons butter

Combine all ingredients except butter. Pour into uncooked pie shell. Add butter in pats over top of mixture. Cover with lattice crust. Bake at 450°F for 10 minutes. Reduce heat to 350°F and continue baking for 40 to 50 minutes, until crust is golden and filling holds shape. Let pie cool and refrigerate until firm.

*

Lemon Cream Pie

"Rich and delicious. Similar to Key Lime Pie."
Judith Parker Vander Salm

Serves: 8
Bake crust: 6 to 8 minutes at 375°F

Graham Cracker Crust

- 20 graham crackers
- ¼ cup confectioners' sugar
- ¼ cup butter, softened

Filling

- 1 14-ounce can sweetened condensed milk
- ½ cup lemon juice
- Grated rind of 1 lemon
- ½ cup whipping cream

To make crust, crush graham crackers and blend with sugar and butter. Mold into 9 x 9-inch pan. Bake at 375°F for 6 to 8 minutes. Cool 5 minutes.

Blend together condensed milk, lemon juice, and lemon rind. Pour lemon mixture into graham cracker crust. Whip cream to soft peaks, sweeten slightly with confectioners' sugar, and pour over top. Refrigerate until ready to serve.

*

Lemon Ice Cream Pie

"Fresh lemon is essential."
Barbara T. Dunn

Serves: 6 to 8
Refrigerate
Bake: 3 minutes at 500°F

- 6 tablespoons butter, melted and cooled
- ⅓ cup lemon juice
- ¾ to 1 cup sugar
- Dash salt
- 2 whole eggs plus 2 egg yolks, slightly beaten
- 1 pie shell, baked
- 1 pint vanilla ice cream, softened

Meringue

- 2 egg whites, beaten
- ¼ cup sugar
- Dash salt

Combine butter, lemon juice, sugar, and salt. Stir in beaten eggs. Bring to a boil over low heat, stirring constantly. Chill. In cooled pie shell, spread ice cream. Top with chilled lemon filling and freeze. To make meringue, beat egg whites until stiff, then fold in sugar and salt. Spread on top of pie. Bake at 500°F for 3 minutes, or broil until golden. Serve immediately. For variety, make *Lemon Parfaits* by layering ice cream and filling in individual glasses and topping with whipped cream and a cherry.

Bowl of Grapes
Yozo Hamaguchi (Japanese b. 1909)
Mezzotint, 29.5 x 34.5 cm
Gift of Mrs. Helen Sagoff Slosberg, 1969.8

*

Crêpes Normandy

"Apples and spice and everything nice."
Mrs. Henry W. LaJoie

Serves: 10
Bake: 10 to 15 minutes at 350°F

Brandy Crêpes

Yield: 18 to 22

- 3 eggs
- 1 cup flour
- 1 cup water
- 1 tablespoon brandy
- ½ teaspoon salt
- 1 teaspoon sugar

Apple Filling

- ¼ cup butter
- 5 medium cooking apples, peeled and thinly sliced
- ¼ cup brown sugar
- ½ teaspoon cinnamon
- 1 tablespoon brandy, or cognac
- ¼ cup orange juice
- 1 tablespoon grated orange rind
- 2 tablespoons melted butter
- Whipped or sour cream

To make crêpes, combine ingredients in blender jar and blend for about 1 minute. Scrape down sides with rubber spatula and blend for another 15 seconds or until smooth. Refrigerate batter for about 1 hour. Batter has tendency to separate while refrigerated, so stir with spoon or spatula before cooking. Cook on upside-down crêpe griddle or traditional pan.

To make filling, heat butter in large skillet, add apples, and sauté until translucent, stirring frequently. Add brown sugar and cinnamon. Cook until sugar dissolves. Remove from heat. Add brandy, orange juice, and orange rind. Spoon about 2 tablespoons apple mixture on center of 10 cooked crêpes. Fold over. Place in shallow baking pan. Brush with melted butter. Heat in 350°F oven for 10 to 15 minutes. Serve with whipped cream. Note: Refrigerate remaining crêpe batter.

*

Pecan Cups

"Serve with a dollop of whipped cream on top."
Karen Beer

Yield: 24 cups
Bake: 25 minutes at 325°F

Crust

- ½ cup butter
- 1 3-ounce package cream cheese
- 1 cup sifted flour

Filling

- 1 tablespoon butter
- ¾ cup light brown sugar
- 1 egg
- 1 teaspoon vanilla
- Pinch salt
- ½ cup broken pecans

Mix butter, cream cheese, and flour and chill for 15 minutes. Shape into 2 dozen balls. Place in tiny, ungreased muffin tins. Press dough on bottom and sides of tin forming cup.

Blend butter and sugar together. Add egg, vanilla, salt, and pecans. Fill cups with pecan mixture and bake at 325°F for 25 minutes, or until filling is set.

*

Flan (Caramel Egg Custard)

"Slow oven insures creamy texture. Baking a day ahead insures more caramel sauce when unmolded."
Iris Alicia Lanyon

Serves: 10
Bake: 40 minutes for cups or 1 hour for mold at 300°F

- 1¾ cups sugar
- 2 13-ounce cans evaporated milk
- 8 eggs, slightly beaten with pinch salt
- 2 teaspoons vanilla

Melt ½ cup sugar in saucepan, stirring constantly. Pour into 10 custard cups or 1½-quart mold as soon as sugar is melted. Set aside. Heat milk, but do not boil. Add remaining sugar and stir until dissolved. Add milk and vanilla to beaten eggs and stir. Pour into caramelized custard cups or mold. Place in pan filled with 1 inch water and bake at 300°F for 40 minutes for cups or 1 hour for mold.

*

Grapenut Pudding

"A nutritious, not-too-sweet dessert."
The Cookbook Committee

Serves: 6

- 1 envelope gelatin
- ½ cup sugar
- Pinch salt
- ½ cup grapenuts
- ½ cup raisins
- 1 tart apple, peeled and finely chopped
- 9 English walnuts, or pecans, finely chopped
- 1 teaspoon vanilla
- Juice of ½ lemon
- 2 cups boiling water

Topping

- 1 tablespoon sugar
- ½ teaspoon vanilla
- 1 cup all-purpose cream, whipped

Soften gelatin in small amount of cold water. Mix dry ingredients. Stir in vanilla and lemon and add water, stirring well. Add softened gelatin and mix well. Refrigerate to thicken. Stir once after pudding is partially set or fruit and nuts will settle to bottom.

When ready to serve, fold sugar and vanilla into whipped cream. Place portions of pudding in individual dessert dishes and add dollop of topping.

*

Lemon Sponge Dessert

"Refreshing and light after a hearty meal."
Marion S. Fletcher

Serves: 6 to 8

- 1 envelope gelatin
- ½ cup hot water
- Scant ½ cup lemon juice
- 3 eggs, separated
- 1 cup sugar
- 1 sponge cake, broken in bite-sized pieces
- Whipped cream
- Grated lemon rind

Soak gelatin in small amount of cold water and add hot water and lemon juice. Beat egg yolks with sugar. Combine gelatin with egg yolks and cool until partially set but still soft, stirring occasionally. Beat egg whites and fold into mixture. Arrange sponge cake in 7-inch casserole and cover evenly with lemon mixture. Refrigerate until set. Unmold and frost lightly with sweetened whipped cream. Sprinkle grated lemon rind sparsely on top.

Lemon Mousse

"Light, lemony, and elegant."
Ann-Katrine M. Rapp

Serves: 12
Refrigerate: at least 6 hours

- 1 package unflavored gelatin
- ½ cup cold water
- 7 eggs, separated
- ¾ cup fresh lemon juice (4 lemons)
- 1½ cups sugar

Dissolve gelatin in water. Set aside. In heavy saucepan, mix egg yolks, lemon juice, and ½ sugar. Cook over medium heat for 8 to 10 minutes, stirring constantly, until thick and smooth. Do not boil. Remove from heat and add gelatin. Set aside. Beat egg whites, adding remaining sugar gradually, and beating thoroughly between each addition, until peaks form and whites are hard and smooth. Fold lemon mixture into egg whites a little at a time. Fold gently until well mixed. Pour into 2½-quart serving dish and refrigerate at least 6 hours. May be frozen 1 day ahead and removed 2 hours before serving. Serve plain or with any fruit sauce.

Orange Sponge Custard

"Creamy and rich."
Mrs. Michael J. Bradbury

Serves: 6
Bake: 35 to 45 minutes for cups or 1 hour for dish at 350°F

- ¾ cup sugar
- 1½ tablespoons butter
- 3 eggs, separated
- Grated rind of 1 orange
- 3 tablespoons flour
- ⅓ cup orange juice
- 1 cup milk

Preheat oven to 350°F. Cream sugar and butter. Beat egg yolks and add with orange rind to butter. Mix thoroughly. Stir in flour, alternating with orange juice and milk. Beat egg whites until stiff but not dry. Fold ½ cup whites into yolk mixture. Then fold yolks into remaining whites.

Place batter in 6 buttered custard cups or 7-inch, ovenproof dish. Set in pan filled with 1 inch hot water. Bake for 35 to 45 minutes for cups or 1 hour for baking dish, or until set. Serve hot or cold.

Salisbury Street Fudge

"Not as rich as cooked fudge."
Dorothy E. Petralis

Serves: 16
Refrigerate: at least 4 hours

- 2 3-ounce packages cream cheese
- 4 cups sifted confectioners' sugar
- 4 ounces unsweetened chocolate, melted
- 2½ teaspoons vanilla extract
- 1 cup chopped walnut meats

In bowl, cream the cheese. *Slowly* blend in sugar and chocolate. Blend in vanilla and nuts. Press into *well-greased* 8 x 8-inch pan. Refrigerate for at least 4 hours. Cut into squares.

*

Macaroon-Pear Dessert

"Serve warm while macaroons are crunchy."
Janice Harwood

Serves: 4
Bake: 15 to 20 minutes at 425°F

- 1 16-ounce can pear halves
- ⅔ cup vermouth
- ⅔ cup apricot jam
- 4 stale macaroons
- ½ cup butter, melted

Drain pear halves and arrange in buttered, shallow, 4 x 8-inch casserole. Mix vermouth and jam until smooth and pour over pears. Crumble macaroons over top and drizzle with melted butter. Bake at 425°F for 15 to 20 minutes. Note: Can be made ahead and heated at last minute.

*

Russian Cream

"Not too sweet and very different."
Nancy Laird

Serves: 6 to 8
Refrigerate: 4 to 6 hours

- ¾ cup sugar
- ½ cup water
- 1 envelope unflavored gelatin

- 1 cup whipping cream
- 1½ cups sour cream
- 1 teaspoon vanilla

Berry Sauce

- 2 cups fresh berries
- ¼ cup sugar
- 1 teaspoon lemon juice
- 1 tablespoon cornstarch
- ¼ cup water

In small saucepan, combine sugar, water, and gelatin and blend well. Let stand 4 to 5 minutes. Place over medium heat and bring to a boil, stirring constantly. Remove from heat. Gradually blend in cream. In medium bowl, combine sour cream and vanilla. Gradually add hot mixture, whisking constantly until smooth. Pour into 6 or 8 wine glasses or dessert dishes. Cover and refrigerate 4 to 6 hours.

For sauce, bring berries and sugar to a boil and add lemon juice. Thicken slightly with mixture of cornstarch and water. Cool before adding to glasses. Note: If using frozen raspberries, leave out sugar.

*

Pavé au Chocolat

"You must work quickly."
Mrs. Jacques J. Burguet

Serves: 6
Refrigerate: at least 3 hours

- ½ cup butter
- ¾ cup sifted confectioners' sugar
- 4 egg yolks
- 4 ounces unsweetened chocolate, melted
- ¼ cup cognac
- ¾ cup water
- 24 ladyfingers

Cream butter in mixing bowl. Gradually add sugar and beat until fluffy. Blend in egg yolks 1 at a time. Stir in melted chocolate. In separate bowl, combine cognac and water. Dip ladyfingers quickly in this mixture, removing at once, and place 8 in a row on oblong platter. Cover with coating of chocolate mixture. Repeat with 2 more layers using ⅓ chocolate. Cover top and sides with remaining chocolate and chill at least 3 hours.

*

Peanut Brittle Meringue

"Elegant."
Frances Dewey

Serves: 8 to 10
Bake: 1 hour at 250°F

- 4 egg whites, at room temperature
- 1 cup fine granulated sugar
- 2 teaspoons vanilla
- 1 8-ounce box peanut brittle
- 1 pint heavy cream, whipped

Beat egg whites until stiff and dry. Beat in 12 tablespoons sugar, 1 tablespoon at a time, until mixture holds shape. Add 1 teaspoon vanilla. Fold in remaining sugar. Grease 2 round cake tins and set round of waxed paper into each tin. Grease paper. Divide meringue evenly between pans and bake at 250°F for 1 hour. Remove from pans while still warm and peel off paper. Turn off oven and set meringues on cookie sheet in oven to dry out. Break up peanut brittle in cloth with wooden mallet. Add remaining vanilla to cream and whip. Place 1 meringue on serving platter. Layer with ½ whipped cream and ½ brittle. Repeat with remaining ingredients. Note: Meringue can be made ahead and will keep in tightly closed tin for several weeks.

*

Swedish Cream Framboise

"Lovely spring-looking dish."
The Cookbook Committee

Serves: 8 to 10
Refrigerate: 3 to 4 hours

- 24 ladyfingers
- 3 to 4 tablespoons Grand Marnier
- 1 envelope gelatin
- 2 cups heavy cream
- 1 cup sugar
- 2 cups sour cream
- 1 teaspoon vanilla
- Frozen raspberries

Line serving dish with ladyfingers and sprinkle with Grand Marnier. In saucepan, cook gelatin, cream, and sugar over medium heat until gelatin is dissolved. Cool mixture until slightly thickened. Stir in sour cream and vanilla. Pour over lady fingers and chill at least 3 to 4 hours. Serve with partially thawed frozen raspberries.

*

Ice and Snow

"Light dessert after a heavy meal."
Mrs. David J. Milliken

Serves: 10

- 1 quart vanilla ice cream
- 1 quart pineapple sherbet
- 3 tablespoons Cointreau, or Triple Sec
- 3 tablespoons Grand Marnier
- 2 teaspoons grated orange rind
- 2 teaspoons grated lemon rind

Combine all ingredients in large bowl and beat just until smooth. When mixture is smooth, spoon into large, stemmed wine or champagne glasses. Mixture will be soft, like old-fashioned ice cream. Store in freezer. Crushed cookie crumbs or grated chocolate may be sprinkled over top for decoration before serving.

Bowl of Fruit, 1918
Diego Rivera (Mexican 1886–1957)
Graphite, 23.5 x 31.1 cm
Museum purchase, 1928.1

*

Mocha Pot de Créme

"Very delicious and so easy."
Jeannette M. Bonneau

Serves: 8
Refrigerate

- 12 ounces dark sweet chocolate
- 1½ cups strong coffee
- 2 tablespoons sugar
- Large pinch salt
- 2 eggs
- 2 teaspoons vanilla extract
- ¼ cup Grand Marnier (optional)

Using double boiler, melt chocolate in ½ cup coffee. While chocolate cools, combine sugar, salt, eggs, and vanilla in blender. Bring remaining coffee to a boil and add to blender with melted chocolate and Grand Marnier. Cover and blend 1 minute. Pour into 8 pots de créme or demitasses and chill in refrigerator until time to serve. May be served with whipped cream.

*

Chocolate Toblerone Mousse au Blanc

"Elegant and simple dessert."
Dieter H. Buehler

Serves: 6
Refrigerate: 3 to 4 hours

- 2 3-ounce packages Toblerone Blanc white chocolate
- 4½ tablespoons water
- 1½ cups heavy cream
- 2 egg whites
- 1 ounce Toblerone milk chocolate, grated

Melt Toblerone Blanc with water over gentle heat or double boiler. Stir until chocolate forms smooth paste. Remove from heat and let stand to cool. Meanwhile, whip heavy cream until stiff. Do not add sugar. Whip egg whites until they stand in peaks. Fold cooled white chocolate evenly into whipped cream. Fold in egg whites thoroughly. Transfer to serving dish. Sprinkle grated milk chocolate over top of bowl. Cover with plastic wrap and refrigerate 3 to 4 hours. Keep cool until ready to serve.

*

Sautéed Apples with Rum Sauce

"Attractive, easy, delicious."
Mrs. Harry E. Goll

Serves: 8

Sauce

- 6 large egg yolks
- 1 cup whipping cream
- 1 cup milk
- ½ cup sugar
- 3 tablespoons dark rum
- 2 teaspoons vanilla

Apples

- 6 tablespoons butter
- 8 apples, peeled, cored, and halved or sliced
- ¾ cup raisins, or to taste
- ⅓ cup sugar
- 1 teaspoon grated lemon rind
- ½ teaspoon cinnamon
- ¼ teaspoon nutmeg

Combine yolks, cream, milk, and sugar in top of double boiler over simmering water. Cook, stirring frequently, until sauce thickens and coats spoon, about 30 minutes. Remove from heat and stir in rum and vanilla. Chill.

Melt butter in large skillet. Add remaining ingredients and sauté over medium heat until apples are soft but not falling apart. Serve warm with chilled sauce.

*

Sorbet de Fraises

"A refreshing, summery treat."
Diane Ryan Kunkler

Serves: 6 to 8

- 1½ cups ripe strawberries, hulled and cleaned
- ¾ cup superfine sugar
- ⅜ cup water
- Juice of 1 orange
- Juice of 1 lemon
- Cream
- Kirsch

Purée strawberries in food processor or blender. Strain through fine sieve to remove seeds. Set aside in large bowl. Cook sugar in water to thread stage over medium heat, or boil exactly 5 minutes. Pour over berries. Mix well and let cool. Add orange and lemon juices, mixing well. Pour into metal trays that have been washed with baking soda and freeze until almost solid. Beat well and return to freezer trays. Serve with cream whipped with kirsch.

*

Blueberry or Raspberry Slump

"An easy, delicious dessert to make after berry picking."
Mrs. Nicholas R. Cowenhoven

Refrigerate: at least 2 hours

- Berries
- Sugar
- Butter
- White bread (Arnold or Pepperidge Farm), crusts removed
- Heavy cream, or vanilla ice cream

Simmer berries with sugar to taste until juice runs and berries are soft. Butter slices of white bread. Put layer of bread in serving dish and pour on berries and juice. Continue alternating layers, being sure that bread gets saturated. Refrigerate 2 or more hours. Serve with heavy cream or vanilla ice cream.

*

Bananas Foster

"Very rich."
Thomas J. Vander Salm

Serves: 2

- ½ cup brown sugar
- Several dashes cinnamon
- 2 tablespoons butter
- 1½ ounces banana liqueur
- 1 ripe banana
- 1 ounce rum
- Vanilla ice cream

In frying pan, melt sugar, cinnamon, and butter over low heat. Blend in banana liqueur. Slice banana lengthwise or crosswise, add to mixture, and cook until very tender. Add rum and flame mixture. When fire dies out, pour or ladle over vanilla ice cream in serving dishes.

*

Curried Fruit

"Guests always want the recipe."
Janet N. Friedell

Serves: 8
Bake: 1 hour at 350°F

- 1 20-ounce can pineapple slices or chunks in syrup
- 1 30-ounce can peach halves
- 1 20-ounce can apricot halves
- ¾ cup butter, melted
- ½ cup brown sugar
- ¼ teaspoon ground cloves
- ¼ teaspoon cinnamon
- 1 teaspoon curry powder

Drain fruit well. Arrange in layers in deep baking dish. Combine butter, sugar, and spices. Spoon over fruit. Bake at 350°F for 1 hour. Serve hot with vanilla ice cream.

*

Butterscotch Sauce

"For homemade sundaes."
Christina Callahan

Yield: 2½ cups

- 1 cup sugar
- ⅞ cup light corn syrup
- ½ cup butter
- 1 cup heavy or all-purpose cream
- 1 teaspoon vanilla

Cook sugar, corn syrup, butter, and ½ cup cream over medium heat in heavy saucepan until it reaches soft ball stage. Add remaining cream. Cook, stirring, until mixture sheets from spoon. Add vanilla and cool. Keep refrigerated, but serve warm.

*

Marshmallow-Mint Sauce

"Delicious on ice cream."
The Cookbook Committee

Yield: 1 cup

- ½ cup sugar
- ¼ cup water
- 8 marshmallows, cut in small pieces
- 1 egg white
- 1 drop oil of peppermint
- Green food coloring

Boil sugar and water for 5 minutes and add marshmallows. Beat egg white until stiff and gradually add marshmallow mixture. Add flavor and coloring and chill.

*

World's Best Hot Fudge Sauce

"Good with ice cream or cream puffs."
Ann T. Ward

Yield: 1¾ cups

- 1 cup heavy or light cream
- 6 tablespoons butter
- ⅔ cup sugar
- ⅔ cup dark brown sugar, firmly packed
- Pinch salt
- 1 cup cocoa

Place cream and butter over moderate heat. Stir until butter melts and cream comes to a low boil. Add sugars and stir to dissolve completely. Test for sweetness. Reduce heat, add salt and cocoa, and stir with wire whisk until smooth. Note: When reheating, add hot water 1 tablespoon at a time. Best reheated in microwave oven.

Afternoon Tea Party, 1891
Mary Cassatt (American 1844–1926)
Color aquatint and drypoint,
34.6 x 28.3 cm
Bequest of Mrs. Kingsmill Marrs,
1926.201

Cookies and Bars

Pepparkakor Cookies NO

"Especially welcome at Christmas time."
Nancy C. Matson

Yield: 5 dozen
Refrigerate dough: overnight
Bake: 6 to 8 minutes at 350°F

- ¾ cup molasses
- 1 teaspoon ginger
- 1 teaspoon cloves
- 1 teaspoon cinnamon
- 1 cup sugar
- 1 teaspoon cardamom seeds, crushed
- 1 teaspoon grated orange rind
- 2 teaspoons baking soda
- ½ cup butter, melted
- ½ cup vegetable shortening, melted
- 2 eggs, beaten
- Dash salt
- 4 cups flour
- Whole almonds

In saucepan, combine molasses, ginger, cloves, cinnamon, sugar, cardamom, and orange rind and bring to a boil. Remove from heat and add baking soda. Stir until cool. Add butter, shortening, eggs, and salt. Stir in flour until dough is firm. Refrigerate at least overnight. Roll thin and cut with cookie cutters. Top each cookie with an almond. Bake at 350°F for 6 to 8 minutes.

Oh Henry Bars

"Kids love them."
Zabelle D'Amico

Yield: 50 to 60 squares
Bake: 18 minutes at 350°F

- ⅔ cup butter
- 1 cup brown sugar
- 4 cups quick oats
- ½ cup light corn syrup
- 3 teaspoons vanilla
- 1 6-ounce package chocolate chips
- ⅔ cup crunchy peanut butter

Cream butter and sugar. Add oats, corn syrup, and vanilla. Press dough into 9 x 13-inch pan. Bake at 350°F for 18 minutes and let cool. Meanwhile, melt chocolate chips and peanut butter. Spread on top and cut into small squares.

Colossal Cookies

"Hearty."
Roberta L. Aronowitz

Yield: 54 large cookies
Bake: 10 to 12 minutes at 350°F

- ½ cup butter
- 1½ cups sugar
- 1½ cups firmly packed brown sugar
- 4 eggs, beaten
- 1 teaspoon vanilla
- 1 18-ounce jar or 2 cups chunk-style peanut butter
- 1 18-ounce carton old-fashioned or quick oats, uncooked
- 1 6-ounce package semi-sweet chocolate chips
- 2½ teaspoons baking soda

In large bowl, beat together butter and sugars until light and fluffy. Blend in eggs and vanilla. Add peanut butter, oats, chips, and baking soda, mixing well after each addition. Drop by scant ¼ cup dry measure about 4 inches apart on ungreased cookie sheet. Flatten with fork to 2½-inch diameter. Bake at 350°F for 10 to 12 minutes. Cool 1 minute on cookie sheet and remove to wire cooling rack. Store tightly covered.

Gingersnaps

"Light molasses, not overpowering."
Dorothy W. O'Toole

Yield: 4 to 5 dozen
Bake: 8 to 10 minutes at 350°F

- 2 cups all-purpose flour, sifted
- ½ teaspoon salt
- 1 teaspoon cloves
- 1 teaspoon ginger
- 1 teaspoon cinnamon
- 3 teaspoons baking soda
- ¾ cup soft shortening
- 1 cup sugar
- 1 egg, slightly beaten
- ¼ cup light molasses

Sift flour, salt, spices, and baking soda together. Cream shortening until light and fluffy. Gradually add sugar. Blend in egg and molasses and stir in flour mixture thoroughly. Drop heaping teaspoonfuls of dough on ungreased cookie sheet about 2 inches apart. Flatten with fingers and sprinkle with sugar. Bake at 350°F for 8 to 10 minutes. Let stand 1 minute before removing from pan.

Or, roll cookie dough into little balls with hands, roll in granulated sugar, and space 2 inches apart on cookie sheet. Flatten lightly with flat-bottomed glass. Bake only 7 to 8 minutes. They come out nicely shaped and not overly crisp.

Paklava

"Best I've ever had."
Sally R. Trottier

Yield: about 54 pieces
Bake: 30 minutes at 350°F

- 1 cup butter
- 2 tablespoons vegetable shortening
- 1 pound walnuts, chopped
- 1 16-ounce package phyllo dough
- 2 cups sugar
- 1 cup water
- 1 teaspoon lemon juice

Melt butter and shortening together. Have pastry brush, walnuts, and butter ready, and dough thawed. Keep towel over unused portion of dough, as it dries quickly and becomes brittle. Boil sugar in water for 5 minutes. Add lemon juice. Set aside to cool. Using rolling pin, or dowel, roll first sheet of dough into 12 x 18 x 1-inch pan and brush lightly with butter. Lay second sheet on top, butter lightly, and continue until ½ dough has been layered and buttered in pan. Spread walnuts evenly over top layer, and continue as above with remaining dough. Cut into 2-inch diamonds and brush top evenly and generously with butter. Bake at 350°F for 30 minutes. Pour off any excess butter. Pour cool syrup mixture over top of paklava. Serve when cool.

Peanut Butter Sticks

"Good after school snack."
Rebecca B. Crocker

Yield: 2 to 3 dozen
Bake: 10 to 15 minutes at 300°F

- 1 loaf unsliced bread, cut in fingers, crusts removed
- 5 ounces peanut butter
- ⅓ cup oil
- 1 teaspoon salt

Bake fingers and crusts at 300°F for 10 to 15 minutes. Roll crusts into crumbs. Heat peanut butter, oil, and salt. Dip fingers in mixture, cool, and roll in crumbs. Serve warm or freeze.

Marshmallow Brownies

"Great for bridge, husbands, and kids."
Mrs. Neal T. Skillings

Yield: 25
Bake: 25 minutes at 350°F

- ⅓ cup butter
- 2 rounded tablespoons cocoa
- 2 eggs
- 1 cup sugar
- ¾ cup flour
- Pinch salt
- 1 cup walnuts, broken in large pieces
- 16 to 18 marshmallows, halved

Frosting

- ⅓ cup butter
- 2 cups confectioners' sugar
- 2 tablespoons cocoa
- 1 teaspoon vanilla
- Pinch salt
- ¼ cup coffee

Melt butter in 1-quart saucepan. Remove from heat and blend in cocoa, eggs, sugar, flour, salt, and nuts. Pour into greased 8 x 8-inch pan. Bake at 350°F for 20 minutes. Remove from oven, arrange marshmallows on top, and bake for 5 more minutes. Let cool.

To make frosting, combine butter, sugar, cocoa, vanilla, and salt. Add coffee gradually, until mixture is of spreading consistency. Frost brownies, cut into squares, and serve.

Hermits

"A good, spicy cookie."
George E. Wespi

Yield: 3 to 4 dozen
Bake: 9 to 13 minutes at 375°F

- 1½ cups shortening
- 2 cups sugar
- 2 eggs
- ½ cup molasses
- 4 teaspoons baking soda
- ½ teaspoon salt
- 4½ cups flour
- 2 teaspoons cinnamon
- 1½ teaspoons ground ginger
- 1½ teaspoons ground cloves
- 1 cup raisins

In bowl, mix shortening, sugar, eggs, and molasses. In separate bowl, combine baking soda, salt, flour, cinnamon, ginger, and cloves. Add dry ingredients to batter. Add raisins. Wet hands and roll dough into sausage shapes with 1-inch diameters. Squash rolls *very lightly*. Sprinkle with granulated sugar. Bake at 375°F for 9 to 13 minutes until cracked on top. Cracks should remain yellow, looking uncooked. Cool before cutting. Store in airtight container. Note: Do not overbake.

Waldo's Famous Brownies

"Mixing should be done by hand with a wooden spoon."
Wallace F. Whitney, Jr.

Yield: 10 squares
Bake: 45 minutes at 375°F

- 2 ounces unsweetened chocolate, or ⅔ cup cocoa
- ½ cup butter
- 2 eggs
- 1 cup sugar
- 1 teaspoon vanilla
- ½ cup sifted flour
- ½ cup chopped nuts

Melt chocolate with butter over double boiler. Meanwhile, beat eggs and add sugar. Blend in vanilla and flour. Add chocolate and nuts. Pour into greased 8 x 8-inch pan. Bake at 375°F for 45 minutes.

Pecan Sticks

"Magic."
Nancy Hatch

Bake: 10 minutes at 275°F

- Graham crackers
- 1 cup butter
- 1 cup light brown sugar
- 1 cup chopped pecans

Line cookie sheet, about 12 x 18 inches, with graham crackers separated at score marks. Melt butter in saucepan. Add sugar and bring to a boil. Boil exactly 2 minutes. Pour over graham crackers until completely covered. Sprinkle pecans on top. Bake at 275°F for 10 minutes. Cool completely.

Whoopie Pies

"Great for kids."
The Cookbook Committee

Yield: 2 to 2½ dozen
Bake: 10 minutes at 350°F

- 2 cups flour
- 1 teaspoon baking soda
- ¼ teaspoon salt
- ⅓ cup cocoa
- 1 egg
- 1 cup sugar
- ¾ cup milk
- ⅓ cup cooking oil
- 1 teaspoon vanilla

Filling

- ½ cup butter, softened
- 1 cup confectioners' sugar
- 3 heaping tablespoons marshmallow fluff
- 1 teaspoon vanilla

Combine cookie ingredients in bowl and mix thoroughly. Drop by teaspoonfuls onto greased cookie sheet. Bake at 350°F for 10 minutes, or until center springs back when gently pressed. Cool on racks.

To make filling, beat ingredients with electric beater. Spread between 2 cookies sandwich style.

Cappucino Thins

"Especially good for food processors."
Patricia Leonard Bagg

Yield: 5 dozen
Refrigerate: 1 hour
Bake: 8 minutes at 350°F

- 4 ounces sweet chocolate, cut in 1-inch pieces
- ½ cup plus 2 tablespoons sugar
- ½ cup packed brown sugar
- 1 egg yolk
- 1 tablespoon freeze-dried instant coffee
- 1 tablespoon unsweetened cocoa
- 1 teaspoon cinnamon
- ¾ teaspoon salt
- 1 cup unsalted butter, cut in 8 pieces
- 1 cup cake flour
- 1 cup unbleached flour

In processor or mixer, chop chocolate until it resembles coarse meal. Transfer to bowl. In processor, combine sugars, egg yolk, coffee, cocoa, cinnamon, and salt and process 1 minute. Add butter and process 1 minute. Add both flours and chopped chocolate. Process by pulsing on and off just until flour is absorbed. Do not overprocess. Shape dough into 1-inch cylinders. (Dough may be frozen at this point.) Chill until firm, at least 1 hour. Slice in ¼-inch slices and place 1½ inches apart on ungreased cookie sheets. Bake at 350°F for 4 minutes, turn, and continue baking 4 more minutes. Cool on racks.

Pecan Dreams

"Can be stored for several weeks in a tin."
Linda Percell Vadasz

Yield: 3 to 4 dozen
Bake: 30 to 40 minutes at 325°F

- 1 cup softened, not melted, butter
- 4 tablespoons sugar
- 2 teaspoons vanilla
- 2 cups flour
- 2 cups finely chopped pecans
- Confectioners' sugar

Cream butter and sugar. Add vanilla, flour, and pecans. Roll into little balls and place on ungreased cookie sheet. Bake at 325°F for 30 to 40 minutes. Remove from oven and roll in confectioners' sugar. Note: This recipe may be made in food processor.

Still-Life Triptych #2, 1977
Peter Plamondon (American b. 1939)
Oil on canvas, 152.7 x 184.1 cm
Jerome A. Wheelock Fund, 1978.42

Sauces and Condiments

♠

Apricot Chutney

"Try some in chicken salad."
Margery B. Morgan

Yield: scant quart

- 2 cups dried apricots, washed and quartered
- 1 cup golden raisins
- ½ lemon, thinly sliced and quartered
- ½ cup halved, thinly sliced onion
- 2 tablespoons candied ginger, coarsely cut
- 1½ cups dark brown sugar
- ½ cup wine vinegar
- ½ cup tomato juice
- 2 cloves garlic, crushed
- 1½ teaspoons dry mustard
- ⅛ teaspoon hot red pepper sauce
- ½ teaspoon salt
- ½ teaspoon cinnamon
- ½ teaspoon ground cloves
- ½ teaspoon allspice

In heavy saucepan, combine all ingredients. Simmer uncovered over low heat until thickened, about 30 minutes. Stir occasionally during cooking.

♠

English Chutney

"Good with almost anything."
Janice Nall Poe

Yield: 4 or 5 pints
Cook: 3 hours

- 6 large ripe tomatoes
- 6 large sour apples
- 4 medium onions
- 4 red peppers
- 1 pound seedless raisins
- 1 pound light brown sugar
- 1 quart cider vinegar
- 2 tablespoons salt, or to taste
- 2 teaspoons cinnamon
- 2 teaspoons ground ginger

Cut fruit and vegetables into small pieces. Combine all ingredients and cook slowly for 3 hours. Pack into sterilized jars.

Rose Hip Jelly

"A nutritious jelly, rich in vitamin C."
Mrs. Roger Kinnicutt, Jr.

Yield: 5 jelly jars

- 2 quarts rose hips from wild Cape Cod roses (rosa rugosa)
- 5 tart apples, unpeeled and quartered
- 2 lemons, sliced
- 2 teaspoons whole cloves
- Sugar

In kettle, cover rose hips, apples, lemons, and cloves with water. Cook over low heat until soft. Mash. Drain through jelly bag. For each cup of liquid, add 1 cup sugar. Boil briskly until "jelly stage" (when syrup threads from spoon). Pour into sterilized jars, seal with wax, cool, and cover. Serve with cold meat.

Tomato Jelly

"Worth the time it takes to make."
Barbara M. Donahue

Yield: 6 jelly jars
Drain: overnight
Cook: 1 hour and 45 minutes

- 7 pounds tomatoes
- 3 pounds sugar
- 1 pint vinegar
- 1 teaspoon whole cloves
- 2 sticks cinnamon (broken)

Peel and quarter tomatoes. In large pan, simmer 45 minutes without water. Let tomato pulp drain overnight. Discard liquid. To pulp, add sugar, vinegar, and small, tied cloth bag containing cloves and cinnamon. Simmer 1 hour. Remove spice bag. Pour into hot, sterilized jars, seal with wax, cool, and cover. Serve with meats, fowl, and fish as you would mint jelly.

Sweet-Hot Mustard

"Slow cooking is the secret."
Mrs. William W. Knight

Yield: 1½ cups
Let stand: overnight
Cook: about 20 minutes

- 3 ounces dry mustard
- ¾ cup white vinegar
- 1 cup sugar
- 2 egg yolks

In ceramic bowl, mix mustard and vinegar. Let stand overnight. Stir in sugar and egg yolks. In saucepan, heat slowly until thickened, about 20 minutes. During cooking, stir often with whisk. Store in refrigerator.

Lemon Yogurt Salad Dressing

"Only 12 calories per tablespoon."
The Cookbook Committee

Serves: 6 to 8
Yield: about 1 cup

- 1 cup plain yogurt
- 1 teaspoon lemon juice
- 1 teaspoon seasoned salt
- ½ grated lemon rind

Stir together and refrigerate overnight. Variation: May be used as dressing for fish by adding chives, chopped olives, etc.

♠

Spiced Cranberry Sauce

"Spicy and not too sweet."
Sharon C. Davis

Yield: 1 quart
Boil: 10 minutes

- 1½ cups sugar
- ¾ cup water
- ¼ cup lemon juice
- ½ teaspoon grated lemon rind
- ½ teaspoon ginger
- ½ teaspoon nutmeg
- 3 cloves
- 1 stick cinnamon
- 1 pound cranberries

In saucepan, combine sugar, water, lemon juice, rind, and spices. Boil for 5 minutes. Remove cinnamon and cloves. Add cranberries. Boil 5 minutes or until skins pop open. Cool. Refrigerate until served.

♠

Strawberry Jam

"Quick and 'messless': 1 bowl, 1 cup, 1 spoon."
Janet S. Jones

Yield: 5½ jelly jars

- 1½ 20-ounce bags large frozen strawberries
- 2 tablespoons water
- 2½ tablespoons powdered fruit pectin
- 3 cups sugar
- Powdered cloves, or cinnamon (optional)

Thaw berries. (In microwave oven, thaw on high for 6 minutes in bags or bowl. Turn bags over or stir after 3 minutes.) In bowl, stir well to break up large berries. Crush lightly but do not mash. Add water and pectin and mix well. In uncovered pan, bring to a rolling boil and boil 1 minute. Stir, add sugar, and stir well. Bring back to a boil over high and boil 1 more minute. Cool 5 minutes. Skim foam and pour into sterilized jelly jars. Stir dash cloves into each jar for unique, spicy flavor. Seal with wax, cool, and cover.

♠

Hollandaise Hughes

"Lower in calories than the regular recipe."
Emma King Peterson

Yield: 2 cups

- 2 tablespoons butter
- 1½ tablespoons flour
- 1 cup boiling water
- ½ teaspoon salt
- 2 egg yolks, beaten until thick
- 1 tablespoon chopped parsley
- 1 tablespoon grated onion
- Juice 1 lemon

In saucepan, melt butter. Stir in flour, boiling water, and salt. Whisk over low heat until thick. Whisk in egg yolks, parsley, onion, and lemon juice. Serve with broccoli, asparagus, or other vegetables.

Fabulous French Dressing

"Especially good with avocado."
Mrs. H. Paul Buckingham III

Yield: about 1½ cups

- ½ cup sugar
- ¼ cup vinegar
- 1 tablespoon lemon juice
- 1 small onion, grated
- 1 small clove garlic, chopped
- 2 tablespoons ketchup
- ½ cup oil
- 1 teaspoon paprika
- 1 teaspoon salt

Mix all ingredients and chill before serving.

Bleu Cheese Dressing

"Good tasting."
Virginia C. Glazier

Serves: 6 to 8
Yield: 2 cups

- ¼ pound Roquefort cheese, crumbled
- 1 cup sour cream
- ¼ cup mayonnaise
- ¼ cup sherry
- ¼ cup wine vinegar
- 1 tablespoon grated onion
- ½ teaspoon salt
- ½ teaspoon garlic salt
- ¼ teaspoon paprika
- Pepper to taste

Mix all ingredients and refrigerate.

Chicago Sauce for Artichokes or Raw Vegetables

"Good and easy."
The Cookbook Committee

Yield: about 1½ cups
Refrigerate: at least 3 to 4 hours

- 1 cup mayonnaise
- 1 teaspoon mustard
- 1 teaspoon Worcestershire sauce
- Dash Tabasco
- 2 tablespoons chopped parsley
- 2 tablespoons vinegar
- ½ clove garlic, minced
- 1 tablespoon capers (optional)
- 2 hard-boiled eggs
- 1 tablespoon minced onion

Put all ingredients into blender and mix until smooth. Serve after chilling 3 to 4 hours or overnight.

Sweet-and-Sour Dressing

"Delicious on fruit salads."
The Cookbook Committee

Yield: about 2 cups

- ¼ cup sugar, or less, to taste
- ½ teaspoon salt
- ½ teaspoon celery salt
- ½ teaspoon white pepper
- ¼ teaspoon dry mustard
- 1 teaspoon salad herbs (basil, chives, garlic, dill)
- 1 teaspoon parsley
- 1 teaspoon paprika
- ½ cup wine vinegar
- 1 cup olive oil

Put dry ingredients into jar, then add vinegar and oil. Shake well and refrigerate.

Mayfair Dressing

"Nice flavor."
Susan Sherer

Yield: about 2 cups

- 1 medium onion
- 1 clove garlic
- 1 heaping teaspoon Accent
- 1 heaping teaspoon mustard
- 1 heaping teaspoon pepper
- 3 tablespoons lemon juice
- 1 2-ounce can anchovy fillets
- 2 eggs
- 1½ cups oil

Mix all ingredients, except eggs and 1 cup oil, in blender. Add eggs and blend. Add remaining oil and blend again. May be thinned with hot water if dressing is too thick. Refrigerate.

Pesto

"An Italian herb sauce."
The Cookbook Committee

Yield: 2 cups

- 1½ cups packed fresh basil leaves
- 2 cloves garlic, cut
- ¼ cup pine nuts, or walnuts, or combination
- ¼ cup grated Parmesan cheese
- ½ cup olive oil

In processor, combine and mix all ingredients, or chop finely, then mash to form paste. Use immediately or freeze. Can be doubled.

♠

Green Butter

"A terrific combination of flavors."
The Cookbook Committee

Yield: ¾ cup
Cook: about 10 minutes

- 7 tablespoons lightly salted butter
- 4 scallions, finely chopped
- 8 watercress stems, chopped
- ½ cup parsley, chopped
- ½ cup spinach, cooked and well chopped
- 2 tablespoons fresh dill
- ½ lemon rind, grated

In small saucepan, melt 1 tablespoon butter. Cook scallions until soft and remove. In same pan, cook watercress until wilted, tossing over high heat for 3 to 5 minutes. In small bowl, mix scallions, watercress, parsley, spinach, dill, and lemon rind. In food processor with metal blade, or in small bowl, beat remaining butter until soft and light. Gently mix in greens. Serve with spinach-stuffed shells or poached fish.

♠

Quick Curry Mayonnaise

"Food processor mayonnaise, plus."
Joan B. Dean

Yield: 1 cup

- 1 large egg, room temperature
- 5 teaspoons lemon juice
- 1½ teaspoons curry powder
- 1 teaspoon Dijon mustard
- 1 small clove garlic, mashed
- ¼ teaspoon salt
- ¼ teaspoon white pepper
- 1 cup olive oil

In food processor, combine all ingredients except olive oil. Mix well. Slowly add oil while mixing.

♠

French-Canadian Stuffing

"For Thanksgiving dinner."
Barbara B. Bessette

Yield: fills 12 to 15 pound turkey

- 5 pounds potatoes
- 1 pound sausage
- 1 pound ground beef
- 2 medium onions, chopped
- Salt and pepper to taste
- ¾ teaspoon poultry seasoning
- Turkey broth (optional)

Peel potatoes and boil until done. Mash coarsely. Prepare sausages according to package directions. Drain and mash into small pieces. Brown beef with onions. Drain off fat. Combine sausage, beef, and potatoes. Add salt, pepper, and poultry seasoning. Moisten with small amount of turkey broth if needed. Pack lightly into turkey.

Bread-and-Butter Pickles

"Good all by themselves."
Sarah Cederbaum Ribeiro

Yield: 8 pints

- 32 4-inch cucumbers, or 52 3½-inch cucumbers
- 8 small onions
- 1 green pepper
- 1 sweet red pepper
- ½ cup coarse salt
- 5 cups sugar
- 1 teaspoon cinnamon
- 1 teaspoon curry powder
- 1½ teaspoons turmeric
- ½ teaspoon ground cloves
- 3 teaspoons mustard seed
- 3 teaspoons celery seed
- 5 cups cider vinegar

Thinly slice vegetables. Add salt, cover with cracked ice, and let stand 3 hours, stirring occasionally. Drain and put in large preserving kettle. Combine rest of ingredients and pour over vegetables. Bring to a boil. Pack into hot, sterilized jars, and seal.

Hot Sauce for Hors d'Oeuvres

"Definitely not for the faint of heart."
Merle R. Ingraham, M.D.

Yield: 1½ quarts
Simmer: 30 minutes

- 2 medium onions, chopped
- 4 to 6 cloves garlic
- 3 tablespoons cooking oil
- 1 16-ounce can tomatoes, chopped
- 1 12-ounce can tomato paste
- 1 to 1½ tablespoons hot pepper flakes
- 1 tablespoon peppercorns
- 2 teaspoons celery salt
- 1 teaspoon oregano
- 1 teaspoon basil
- 1 tablespoon monosodium glutamate (optional)

In 2-quart saucepan, sauté onions and garlic in oil. Add tomatoes, tomato paste, hot pepper flakes, peppercorns, celery salt, oregano, basil, and monosodium glutamate. Bring to a boil, lower heat, and simmer, uncovered, for 30 minutes. Note: Gets hotter if prepared a day or two ahead. Especially good served with hot, fried, breaded shrimp and Bent's common cracker halves. Also recommended as dip for tostados or taco chips.

Horseradish Mousse

"Wonderful with roast beef sandwiches."
Rebecca B. Crocker

Yield: ¾ cup

- ½ cup whipping cream
- 3 tablespoons well-drained horseradish
- ¼ teaspoon salt
- 2 teaspoons grated onion
- 1 teaspoon lemon juice

Whip cream and gently fold in horseradish, salt, onion, and lemon juice. Chill.

Index

Master Pastry Cook (Franz Bremer, Cologne), 1928
August Sander (German 1876–1964)
Gelatin-silver print, 29.5 x 21.1 cm
Sarah C. Garver Fund, 1975.118

T

V

W

Y

Z